ADVENTURES

OF A

NANNY

A TRUE STORY

May 2012

To Wykete,
Best wishes
Rachel Kendal

BY

RACHEL KENDAL

Rainbow Associates
Cincinnati, Ohio
USA

Also by Rachel Kendal:

Following My Dreams
with the
Edgar Cayce Readings

Available at Amazon.com

www.rachelkendal.webs.com

Contact

markkeillor@hotmail.com

ACKNOWLEDGEMENTS

My sincere thanks go to my dear friend, Jane Bentz, for typing my manuscript, and to Tony Hollin for proofreading it.

My deep appreciation goes to Mark Keillor, a fellow writer, for helping me to self-publish this book, and for the many laughs we had while doing so.

I dedicate this book to all the children whom I've helped to grow up in a loving environment. I'll always remember them.

Dear Reader:

Adventures of a Nanny is an overview of the 28 years I spent with children in various locales, teaching them how to grow up, and to be happy while doing so. We laughed every day because life is so funny! I wrote this book over a four-year period after I retired and had time to sift through my memories, notes, and pictures of the fun times we had together. The cartoons depict the afterthoughts I had after writing certain paragraphs. My problem with drawing was that I didn't know how to draw. So I started out with stick figures, skinny legs, and triangle skirts. My artistic abilities improved slightly as time went on, until the last cartoon in the book actually looks like me and the boys.

You will be able to identify me in the cartoons by the three wild curls hanging down the back of my neck. In damp weather my hair turns into uncontrollable corkscrews. I hope you get as much enjoyment from reading this book as I did writing it. So fasten your seat belts and get ready to travel through every-day life with a laugh.

Rachel

ADVENTURES OF A NANNY

CHAPTER 1

In 1982 I moved to Washington, DC and lived with my daughter, Shelley, for a month while looking for a teaching job.   Since there was nothing available that interested me, the employment counselor suggested I take a nanny job which required caring for a two-year-old boy while traveling with his parents in Italy and Israel. I was very interested! It paid more than a teacher's salary and all travel expenses were included. I was ready to go!

I met two-year-old Dino Ben-Gurion and his parents the next day and we liked each other immediately. I moved into a small apartment in their attic the following week, and we started packing for a month-long vacation. We were going to visit Italian grandparents in Italy and Jewish grandparents in Israel.

In a happy mood, we flew out of Dulles Airport at midnight. Dino stretched out on two seats with his brown bear, sippy cup and binky (pacifier) and fell asleep immediately.   I covered him with his blankey (small blanket), and found a travel magazine to read. I was too excited to sleep. Mom and Dad were sitting in back of us, sound asleep. (Hereafter, I will refer to the parents of the children I work with as "Mom" or "Dad" to assure their privacy.)   Others were moving around eating, drinking, and talking. About two a.m. I dozed off. A few hours later I woke up when the plane landed in Rome. We rushed to catch another plane to a smaller airport in Lamezia. Breakfast was served and Dino played happily with his toys and books. From the airport, Dad drove us in a rented car to Calabria.

We were greeted by grandparents and various relatives with big hugs, kisses on both cheeks, and lots of tears. Although I'd never been to Calabria before, grandmother looked familiar. She was eighty-five years old and had a large pasta pot. Dino called her Strega Nona, and there was a guy named Big Anthony cutting the grass in the back yard. It seemed to me I had been there before. Could I have stepped into some sort of time warp in one of Tomi De Paolo's children's books?

For lunch, Strega Nona had a big platter of spaghetti and meatballs ready for us. Dino started yelling that he wanted Matzo balls. I put him in the high chair and gave him spaghetti and meatballs. He threw his plate on the floor, much to the delight of the dog who gobbled it up in three seconds. I put some peas and Cheerios on the high-chair tray for Dino and he threw them across the room, one at a time. The dog also ate them. (He was probably an international gourmet.) The mess on the floor was no problem because Strega Nona wasn't a fussy housekeeper. In fact, the floor was so dirty, I could have grown potatoes on it. There was a sign on the kitchen door which read:

Come on in, sit down, converse.
My house doesn't always
Look like this,
Sometimes it's even worse.

Mom tried to feed Dino some soup and he threw it on the floor (more dog food). Strega Nona gave him a raisin bun. He picked out the raisins, ate them, and threw the bun out the window, yelling, "I want linguini and potato pancakes." Dad came in and offered him an apple. He threw it at the dog and screamed, "I want pizza and lamb shanks." Big Anthony came in and gave Dino a peach. He hit Big A on the head with the peach and yelled, "I want breadsticks and corned beef." Big A said, "Dino doesn't know if he wants to eat Italian or Jewish." Big A tried to entertain him by singing, *Head and Shoulders, Knees and Toes,* and going through the motions. As he was bending over to touch his toes, the dog ran over and bit a finger out of his work glove. I said, "That's enough Big A, the dog is trying to tell you you're no Michael Jackson."

I took Dino out of the high chair and placed him on the floor. He ran to the cupboard, got a sharp knife and ran toward his dad. Dad fainted and Dino ran out the door with Big A chasing him. Strega Nona came into the kitchen, poured a pitcher of water on Dad's head and said, "Get up. We're going to the market of the fleas. I got a boy scout to help Big A babysit Dino. He can tie knots, start a campfire, iron his uniform and polish his shoes. I think he can manage a dirty diaper." I told Big A that if Dino tried to jump off the balcony to whisper "cookie" and that would stop him.

As I was rummaging through articles at the flea market, I felt someone pinch my thigh. I turned around to see an Italian man less than five feet tall smiling at me and saying, "Bella, Bella." I said, "Get lost sicko before I give you a bell-shaped head." He backed off. After we went back home I got three more offers from short Italian men. The delivery man said, "Bella bambina, how about going out to lunch with me?" I slammed the door in his face. The telephone repairman said, "I gotta your number, bambina." The pest control man said, "I sure like to bugga you, bambina." I think short men like me because I am five-feet, two-inches tall, and weigh one-hundred and ten pounds. But I am no pushover.

It was day three of our trip and I was exhausted. Dino was very energetic, didn't take naps and woke up every two hours during the night yelling for cookies, his sippy cup or his binky. He could outrun me when it was time for a diaper change. I had to chase him through the house armed with a clean diaper, three baby wipes, and a tube of butt balm, shouting, "Come here, you little imp!" His sturdy little legs kept running as his black curls bounced on his head. He was adorable. Could I take a month of this activity? Was my problem jet lag or Dino?

After spending five hectic days in Calabria, we flew to Milan to attend cousin Gina's wedding. We stayed in Milan for the three days prior to the wedding and Grandpa Guido took us sightseeing. He was proud of Milan, his birthplace, and although I couldn't understand Italian, I saw the love in his eyes when he said, "Me-lawn-o." So I started pronouncing Milan his way. He took us on a subway to Milan's Church of Santa Marie delle Grazie where Leonardo Da Vinci had painted *The Last Supper* on the wall from 1494 to 1498. We watched two artists restoring an area where time had not been kind to the painting. Dino had no interest in art and was so noisy that a guard told him to be quiet. I took him outside for a walk. Later Mom came out and walked with him while Grandpa and I watched the artists at their work. (A thought: While Da Vinci was painting this beautiful and meaningful mural, Columbus was sailing to the New World.)

We had lunch, and then went to visit an ancient castle. My imagination ran wild as I tried to envision myself as a nanny to children in a castle. Dino ran through many rooms and up and down stone steps, almost falling into the moat. I finally put him in his stroller with a tight seat belt and he fell asleep. Mom and I visited some gift shops while Grandpa sat on a bench and watched Dino sleep. We were tired when we went home. Dino slept well that night and so did I.

At 9:30 a.m. the next morning we were at the church for the wedding. The bride was beautiful, the groom handsome, and everybody was happy. There were lots of tears but nobody fainted. After the ceremony, about two-hundred people drove to Bergamo for the reception. Dad was driving Grandpa's ten-year-old Fiat. After an hour of speeding on the freeway, which had no speed limit, the car made odd noises and we stopped to get it checked. It took an hour for repairs and Dino was restless. We went to a coffee bar where Dino had cookies and orangino and I had espresso. Then we went for a

walk in the meadow and Dino picked a bouquet of red poppies for his mommy. When he handed it to her, she shed a tear at his thoughtfulness and he kissed her cheek. We finally got back on the road.

We arrived at Da Mimmo's Restaurant in Bergamo a half hour later. As we entered, Dino spied a suit of armor and yelled "Robot" as he ran toward it. I ran after him and grabbed his hand before he could touch it. After many hugs and double kisses, Uncle Mimmo (the bride's uncle) announced that the meal was ready and everyone found a seat. After the fifth course, we were served lime gelato and I thought that was dessert until the waiter placed a filet mignon in front of me. I refused it and took Dino outside for a walk. Apparently, the lime gelato was meant to refresh one's palate and get prepared for several more courses of rich food. Dino and I returned to the restaurant an hour later and the groom was stomping the floor yelling, "Mangia! Mangia! Eat! Eat!" I felt as if I didn't want to eat for a week. I was relieved when the dancing started and we began to work off some of those calories.

We stayed at a new hotel which was located near Da Mimmo's. I noticed two indentations shaped like graves in the side yard. I asked the desk clerk what they were and she said they were ancient graves that archeologists were going to open soon. I said, "I hope not while I am here." She laughed at my cowardice.

The following day we explored Bergamo's church buildings and cobblestone streets. In the evening, we joined a street festival with lots of dancing, food and wine. Dino liked wine. I had to watch him carefully because he was after everybody's wine glass, trying to get a sip. About 9:00 p.m. I took him back to the hotel and Mom and Dad stayed to socialize with family and friends.

The next morning we left for Gravanago where we had rented an apartment in an old renovated building which was perched on a hillside. It was originally occupied by farmers who tilled the nearby land. The village had been abandoned during WWII because of repeated bombings. After the war, people started rebuilding and planting vineyards. Now it was a peaceful place to unwind, with three bed and breakfast inns serving the professional people who wanted to get away from the city to relax.

The picturesque view from the kitchen window was breathtaking. As Dino and I sat at the table sipping milk and espresso, we discussed the grapevines that grew in row after row, and snaked their way up the distant hillside, disappearing over the ridge. On another hill we could see a castle, and with binoculars we watched men repairing the outside wall, getting it ready for visitors who wanted a glimpse into an ancient way of life. Dino listened intently as I made up a story of a prince and princess who lived in the castle long ago. As a preschool teacher, I knew endless stories that fascinated small children. Dino was one of the brightest children I'd worked with. He remembered the stories so well that he told them to his friends verbatim.

As we explored Gravanago and became friendly with the neighbors, Dino became attached to a five-year-old girl and liked to hold hands while walking with her. One day while walking with several preschoolers to a hilltop we could see hills in all directions. I pretended to be Julie Andrews. I sang, "The hills are alive with the sound of music!" To our surprise, we heard an echo and the children began to sing. We had so much fun!

Every morning Grandpa Guido got up early and drove about fifteen minutes to Fortunago, a nearby village, to buy a newspaper and fresh-baked focaccia bread for our breakfast. One morning a neighbor, Paola, who lived in a compound down the road, invited us to have lunch with him. I was wary of going inside the seven-foot concrete wall because two Saint Bernard dogs stood at the iron gates staring at us when we walked by. Paola assured us he would tie up the dogs before we got there. So much for good intentions! As we stepped inside the gates, the dogs, which were on a leash tied to a timber, ran toward us dragging the heavy load behind them. I grabbed Dino and ran back through the gates just as Paola got them under control with much Italian cursing. After the dogs were safely locked in the garage we had a delicious lunch. The menu consisted of roast chicken, ravioli, and vegetables from Paola's garden, nuts, fruit, cake, wine and espresso.

Paola, a widower, lived alone (with the dogs) and was happy to have guests to cook for. He spoke English and told us some funny stories about culture clash when he lived in New York City in 1935. He and Grandpa had been friends since they started rebuilding their homes in 1948. I wish we could have spent more time with Paola, but we were scheduled to get Dino baptized in Fortunago the next day. Mom invited Paola to go with us and he readily accepted.

The little old brick church sat on a hill amid numerous flower beds of roses, daises, day lilies, coneflowers and butterfly bushes. Colorful butterflies were clinging to the bushes. It looked like a scene from a fairytale. Dino was impressed with the church bell which he rang by pulling a rope in the vestibule. He was the only child present and he knew something serious was about to happen because we adults were talking with hushed voices. He sat still on Dad's lap. What a treat for me; to see him sit still! The priest emerged from the back of the altar and asked Dino, his parents and godparents to step up to the baptismal font. Dino clung to his dad while the priest was talking and blessing everyone, then suddenly he reached down and slapped the water in the font, splashing the priest. The priest laughed, much to our relief. (A thought: Mom was Roman Catholic; Dad was Jewish. How are they going to reconcile their differences in theological beliefs as Dino gets older? What about the ceremony of the bar mitzvah when Dino reaches age thirteen? I wished them the best.)

We went back to Gravanago to celebrate with dinner, wine and dancing. Several neighbors joined us and the children went wild. Italians sure knew how to have fun. I think the feasting, wine and dancing are a holdover from the activities of the Roman Empire. I danced the polka with every short man in the room.

The next day we left for an overnight visit in Venice. The Fiat made it to the water taxi, which delivered us to Saint Mark's Square. With Dino in his stroller, we absorbed the unique Byzantine atmosphere and viewed the Bridge of Sighs, which connects an old prison to Doge's Palace, the seat of Venice's government for many centuries. We bought glass earrings for Mom and me, and a small glass cup for Dino. Dino was very attentive as we watched the glass-blowing demonstration where Venetian craftsmen fashioned their delicate objects.

It was a beautiful day and people were greeting each other with a smile and a "Boun giorno!" Lunch at the sidewalk café was so delicious that Dad had seconds. I took Dino for a walk and watched him chase pigeons while Mom and Dad had espresso. We meandered down a street that led to the Grand Canal where the gondolas caught Dino's attention. He wanted to ride in the "boat." After more sightseeing, Mom approved of a trip down the Grand Canal, and bargained with a gondolier for a lower price ticket. We sat in two wicker chairs in the gondola, and I held Dino on my lap. Mom asked the gondolier to sing, *O Solo Mio* in Italian for Dino. Dino was wide-eyed and motionless as we moved through the water surrounded by eight other gondolas. After a half-hour ride, we staggered off the gondola in a stupor and sat on a bench to regain our equilibrium. Dino sat there, staring into space.

On a pier nearby, locals sat shoeless, dangling their feet over the edge while taking in the sunset. We slowly wandered back to our hotel, passing street musicians with violins, who were singing Italian love songs.

For centuries, Venice has captivated travelers with an array of romantic images: gondola rides through glistening canals at sunset, homes painted in vibrant hues of periwinkle, pink, yellow and plum. I admired the architecture; but was very concerned that the sea had inundated the lower story of some of the houses and buildings. How much longer could Venice survive? I wondered.

The following morning we ate breakfast at the hotel, then went to mass at Saint Mark's Basilica. Mom sat in the front of the church and received communion. Dad, Dino and I were not Catholics, so we sat quietly in the back and observed the service. After visiting a museum, we bought pizza and gelato from a street vendor, and then headed to the pier where the water taxi took us back to the mainland. The Fiat started running on the first turn of the key, much to our delight, and we were on our way back to Gravanago.

Bad news was awaiting us when we arrived in Gravanago. Uncle Guido informed us that Dad's father in Tel Aviv was very ill; and Dad made plans to fly there immediately. Mom, Dino and I would follow him in three days. However, when Dad called the next day he told us to cancel our trip to Tel Aviv and wait for the crisis to pass. His father had developed pneumonia. Our lives were put on hold for three more days until we got the good news that Dad's father was recovering. Dad advised us to go to Milan for a week, and he would meet us there so we could fly home together. I was disappointed that I wouldn't be able to visit the museums in Israel. I especially wanted to see the *Dead Sea Scrolls* and the *Book of Isaiah.* Hopefully someday I would be able to do so.

Mom drove the Fiat up and down mountains with Grandpa sitting beside her. Dino and I were in the back seat, sitting on the luggage. The road was so narrow in some places that Mom had to pull over to let a truck go by. Dino sat quietly while I told him stories: *The Three Bears, Goldilocks, Rapunzel,* and *Heidi,* who lived in the Alps.

When I did an imitation of *Heidi* yodeling, Grandpa turned around, looked me in the eye, and didn't say anything. I got the message.

Dino pretended to read the books as he turned the pages. Grandpa put a newspaper over his head to block out the sun, hunched down in the seat, and was soon snoring. I envied him, but I had to stay awake with Dino. Mom and I chatted for a few minutes until Dino saw the newspaper on Grandpa's head. He stood up behind Grandpa and slapped the newspaper, eliciting a lot of Italian cursing from the front seat. Mom and I could not contain our laughter.

We finally reached our hotel in Milan. The room was too warm and upon opening a window, two cats walked in. I put them out and started the portable air conditioner which was not quite noisy enough to drown out the sound of a helicopter landing on the roof of a nearby hospital. After we had dinner at a sidewalk café, we settled in for the night. Dino slept with his bear. He hadn't asked for the binky, bottle or blankey for two weeks. He was so distracted by everyday events that he didn't need them.

After breakfast the next morning, we wandered around shops and Mom went into a book store. I sat down on a bench outside with Dino in his stroller. I noticed a group of Japanese tourists conversing nearby. A Japanese man walked up to me and said: "Scuzzi Senor..." I laughed to see a Japanese man speaking Italian. I didn't understand what he said. I put my right hand over my heart and said, "Americana." He said, "Thank you." The group burst into laughter and walked away.

We walked to the Duomo Di Milano and went inside. (A thought: Thank God the cathedral wasn't bombed during WWII.) I was overwhelmed by this beautiful work of art. Mom wanted to light a candle and pray for Dad's father, so I took Dino to the lower level of the cathedral. As we descended the steps, Dino said, "He's sleeping." I looked around the area and saw several corpses in glass coffins. I was stunned! I quickly turned around and took Dino upstairs. So much for my curiosity. I took Dino outside to chase pigeons while I tried to figure out what I had just seen. I was relieved when Dino didn't question me about the corpse he had seen. I couldn't explain that sight to anyone. Later, when I asked Mom about the lower level of the Duomo, she said it contained bodies of revered church officials from past centuries. So much for culture shock. I didn't want to know anymore about the lower level of the cathedral. We went to a coffee bar and I had a double-shot espresso.

Later that afternoon, Grandpa took Dino to his room for a nap while Mom and I went shopping. I loved the Italian fashions. I bought a dress and a pair of shoes. Mom bought four dresses, a jacket, three pairs of shoes and jewelry. She said, "Don't tell Dad!" While we were shopping, Dad called to say he would be in Milan the next day. Mom quickly rented another room for them at the hotel.

The next day I packed for our trip home and Dino, Grandpa, and I spent the afternoon at the park. Grandpa spoke Italian to us, and I smiled a lot, wishing I could understand him. It was a bittersweet afternoon knowing I would probably never see him again. Just before sunset we had dinner at a sidewalk café, and then headed for the hotel. I gave Dino a quick bath and he fell asleep watching television. Mom went to Grandpa's room to catch up on family matters. She made the trip to Italy every four months. They were a close-knit family.

We boarded a plane at the Milan airport at 7:00 p.m. and Grandpa drove the Fiat back to Gravanago. We slept through most of the flight and were glad to be home when we landed at Dulles Airport. Mom asked me to stay with Dino for another week until his nanny returned from vacation. I eased Dino back into his routine: regular meals, nursery school three mornings per week, play dates with his peers and visiting a museum, zoo and park. Dino had forgotten about his binky, bottle and blankey. This was a rite of passage for him; a mission accomplished for me. His nanny was pleasantly surprised at his progress. Dino had not become emotionally attached to me during the five weeks I had cared for him. I knew I would be with him for a short time and did not encourage him to bond with me. His hugs and kisses were directed toward Mom and Dad. My job was that of a teacher, a playmate, a friend—I just enjoyed being with him.

I stayed with my daughter, Shelley, for two weeks while interviewing for another job. I went to two nanny agencies and was offered my pick of seven placements where the families wanted a nanny immediately. Of course I intended to pick the family where the benefits would be most advantageous for me; but the employment counselor told me about two little girls who really needed me. Their parents had been divorced for a year, the girls lived with their dad, and the fourth nanny was ready to leave as soon as they could find another one. I wanted to help them and I signed a one-year contract.

During the twenty-six years I worked as a nanny, I knew many other nannies due to our little charges playing together. Only two of the nannies I have known were capable of handling children's emotional problems. Many of the nannies were frustrated and changed jobs often. I lived with eleven different families in Maryland, Washington, DC, Richmond, VA, Michigan and Northern Virginia. The shortest time I stayed on a job was one year;

the longest period was six years. Some of the children outgrew their need for a nanny. The following chapters explain my reasons for moving on.

ADVENTURES OF A NANNY

CHAPTER 2

The family lived in Potomac, MD less than an hour drive from DC. Dad was a lawyer with an office in DC, and Mom was an unemployed lawyer living nearby. Dad was very worried about the girls, Judy, age 8, and Helen, age 11, because they cried several times a day. They saw their Mom on Wednesday evenings and stayed with her every other weekend. They were doing well in school, but needed some extra-curricular activities. Dad had a cleaning service twice a week for the four-bedroom house. A nice nanny's apartment in the basement had a view of surrounding hills. I agreed to move in on the following weekend so the four of us could get acquainted and make plans for the future.

On Saturday, Dad and the girls helped me move into my apartment, then we went out to lunch and they showed me the neighborhood and the shopping mall. That evening the girls helped me make dinner. Dad was pleased with their friendliness toward me and we got off to a good start. Shady, the sixty-five pound dog of dubious descent, liked me and licked my leg several times. I made a mental note to teach him some manners. On Sunday afternoon the girls did school work, then after dinner watched a movie with Dad before bedtime.

Monday morning it saddened me to see them crying at breakfast. Dad drove them to school and came back to tell me that he was optimistic about their behavior improving with me there. He proceeded to tell me unkind things about his ex-wife. He had locked her out of the house eighteen months previously, and her clothes and personal belongings were still in his bedroom. Shady had outgrown his doghouse a year ago, but it was still in Dad's room. Shady was his "baby" and slept beside his bed. He was allowed to run all over the three-story house except in my apartment. He sprinkled dog hair everywhere; hence, the need for maid service twice a week.

Each of the girls had a bedroom with a caged guinea pig that needed additional care. The three-car garage was half-full of used furniture, and I parked my car in the driveway. The leaves needed to be raked and the yard prepared for winter. The windows were dirty and the draperies were threadbare. The cabinets and closets looked like disaster areas. I felt that I couldn't live/work in such a disorderly environment, and I told Dad I was going to organize the house. He said, "Do anything you want, just try to make the girls happy."

The first thing on my agenda was to get the animals under control. I showed the girls how to clean the guinea pig cages and brush Shady, and they cooperated on a daily schedule. Every time Shady licked my leg, I pinched his ear just enough to get his attention. Within two weeks he no longer licked my leg. I dragged his doghouse down the steps and put it on the deck. When Dad asked me how I moved it, I said, "It levitated." He smiled. I bought a large doggie pillow and placed it in the television room for Shady's afternoon naps which were previously taken on the living room sofa. The upholstery and carpets were cleaned. Windows were cleaned and new draperies were installed. The yard was put in order and the Salvation Army picked up the furniture in the garage.

I tackled the cabinets and closets with a vengeance, and found that some of the food in the pantry was up to three-years beyond the "use by" date; and most of the girls' clothes were too small for them. We enjoyed shopping for new clothes.

After a three-week organizational spree, the house looked great and I decreased the maid service to one day per week. The girls were at school from 9 a.m. until 3 p.m. every day and I had spare time to cook and sew. I cooked their favorite meals and made skirts for them. On weekends we cooked together. All of us started to gain weight and Dad asked me to bake fewer pies and cakes.

We enjoyed the circus, basketball games, school plays, and entertained the girls' friends at home with pajama parties. The after-school swimming and basketball gave them good exercise and they looked healthy. They had stopped crying and appeared to be happier. I made French braids in their long, blonde hair for their piano recital, and we were excited when Helen won first prize in the competition.

I had been totally focused on the girls and house for three weeks and was eager to visit Shelley in Arlington for a three-day weekend while the girls stayed with their Mom. I picked up Shelley early Saturday morning and we headed toward Harper's Ferry, WV to delve into some early American history. Harper's Ferry is famous for the thwarted takeover of the Federal arsenal by John Brown, the abolitionist, in 1859. Located at the junction of the Potomac and Shenandoah Rivers, bordered by West Virginia and Maryland, surrounded by verdant mountains, this peaceful scene belied the tragedy that had occurred there. We sat on park benches and sipped coffee while listening to the tour guide's interesting account of the history of Harper's Ferry. After lunch and a lively discussion with other tourists about slavery in the Old South, we started the drive home. My curiosity pertaining to early American history was satisfied for that day. (For information, Google John Brown + abolitionist.)

On Sunday we invited two girlfriends to lunch and had a great time gossiping. On Monday we lounged at home, ate pizza; then went to Crystal City to shop. After dinner I drove back to Potomac and greeted the girls when they came home smiling with large bags of new clothes.

I was awakened at 7 a.m. the next morning by the ringing telephone. I heard an angry woman's voice say, "Come and get your damn dog. He's in my garbage can again!" I recognized the caller's voice, and I knew she was referring to Shady. She lived about fifty yards down the hill and Shady checked her garbage can daily. Jumping our fence was no challenge for him. But Shady's behavior was a problem for me because I did not want him to upset the neighbors.

I quickly got dressed, looked out the window and saw Shady walking down the street in front of the neighbor's house. I hurried to the kitchen, made a roast beef sandwich with mayo (Shady's favorite), jumped into my car and went after him. As I pulled up beside him and stopped, he ignored me. I got out of the car and showed him the sandwich, trying to entice him into the car. He wasn't interested because he had already eaten breakfast from the garbage can. As he continued down the street I followed him in the car. The fat that he had accumulated from eating garbage can meals made him appear to be wearing three fur coats. He was a big, black, blob plodding along the street. He often jumped the fence and roamed the neighborhood for hours. The neighbors called to report his whereabouts. He was chasing their dog or cat, digging in a flower bed, scratching on their door, sitting on the hood of their car, etc. They considered him the neighborhood nuisance; but all the kids loved him and Shady loved to run and play with them.

Shady went over to the curb and sat down. I parked the car and sat down beside him. I tried to communicate with his blank stare, and slumped over, defeated demeanor; but he wouldn't make eye contact with me. (A thought: This is ridiculous! It's time for my preschool imagination to kick in.)

Shady: "Nobody likes me. I'm going to run away from home."

Rachel: "Where would you go? How would you get food and shelter?"

Shady: "I'll get a job."

Rachel: "You're a dog. Nobody would hire you."

Shady: "I've already got a job."

He handed me a newspaper clipping which read: Secretary wanted, must type, take dictation and speak a foreign language.

Rachel: "Dogs can't type."

Shady: "I type sixty-five words per minute."

Rachel: "Dogs can't take dictation."

Shady: "I do a hundred and twenty words per minute."

Rachel: "Shady, you are out of order! You have a good home; we treat you well, even though you never cooperate. You cause me a lot of grief and embarrassment with the neighbors. Why are you so obstinate? What about that part of the advertisement that says you must speak a foreign language?"

Shady: "I can speak a foreign language."

Rachel: "Shady, I am absolutely flabbergasted by you! Dogs can't speak a foreign language."

Shady: "Yes, I can."

Rachel: "Let me hear you."

Shady: "Meow."

He didn't resist as I grabbed his collar and shoved him into the back seat of the car. When we got home, I watched the morning news on TV. Shady watched me eat his roast beef sandwich. I didn't care what he was thinking.

At dinner that evening, Dad and the girls laughed as I told them about the morning episode with Shady. On a more serious note, we discussed plans for cutting calories before they outgrew their new clothes. We decided to eliminate cake, pies, soda and potato chips from our daily diet, and to eat fruit for snacks until our waistlines were back to normal.

The girls tidied up the kitchen and we played Monopoly for a half hour until Judy (who often beat us) realized she was too far behind to catch up and offered Dad a kiss to let her cheat. Dad refused and she burst into tears and ran to her room. That was a cry from frustration, not sadness. Thus, she learned at age eight that cheating was not acceptable. Even so, she was one up on many adults who had never learned that lesson.

I volunteered to go with Helen's fifth-grade class to Gettysburg National Military Park. We boarded the school bus at 9:00 a.m. for the one-hour ride up Interstate

270 to Frederick, and then onto Route 15, which was a beautiful, scenic drive to our destination.

Upon arrival we watched a movie explaining the historic site, and then ate our brown-bag lunches in the picnic area. We boarded a double-decker bus and toured the battlefield. The children were somber as the guide described the tragic battle that had occurred there during the Civil War. It was a sobering experience for children who had led a sheltered life. There seemed to be an aura of sadness and desolation engulfing all of us, and I was relieved when the tour took us to the nearby farm of General Dwight D. Eisenhower. We especially liked the large, comfortable farm house with two beagles sleeping on the back porch.

On the way back to school, we sang until we were hoarse, then sat quietly and rested. Parents were there to pick up their children, and we all went home pondering our adventure.

The girls left for their walk to school the next morning, and five minutes later Mom called asking me to meet her at the local McDonald's for coffee and conversation. Dad still wouldn't let her come into the house. I figured she wanted to get an update on the girls' welfare; but not so. She told me about her problems with her boyfriend and asked my advice. The boyfriend of six months wanted her to live with him, and she was afraid of doing anything that would jeopardize her getting joint custody of the girls. What would *I* do? I certainly wouldn't live with a man without marriage, I told her. I didn't even want to live with the one I was married to. I am divorced. I encouraged her to speak to her lawyer who was a divorced woman. After a quick cup of coffee I said good-bye and decided not to meet with her again. I knew she was seeing a psychologist twice a week; and Dad was in group therapy for divorced men. I figured my job was to keep the girls living a balanced life, and let their parents dump on the professional psychologists instead of me.

Dad made plans to take the girls to Philadelphia to visit with his parents for a few days during the Thanksgiving holidays, so I had free time to do as I pleased. They left on Wednesday morning and I went to the Kennedy Center in DC to pick up my daughter, Debra, who was a secretary in Sergeant Shriver's office.

I admired Sergeant Shriver as a longtime advocate for the poor. He initiated the Peace Corps, Head Start, VISTA, Special Olympics and other social programs to help the powerless. My work in Detroit's Head Start program was so fulfilling that I knew my purpose in life was to work with children. I started college and four years later received a bachelor's degree in child development and psychology from the University of Michigan. After working several years as a preschool teacher, I found myself working happily as a nanny in Washington, DC.

After lunch Debra and I shopped in Georgetown, and then I drove home. Shady wanted to go for a walk so I attached his leash to his collar and we toured the neighborhood for a half hour.

Later, my friend Anne arrived to spend the night and have Thanksgiving dinner with me the next day. Anne and I were members of Edgar Cayce's Association for Research and Enlightenment (A.R.E.) located in Virginia Beach, VA, and we were making plans to give a series of lectures introducing others in the Gaithersburg/Rockville, MD area to the A.R.E. We solidified our plans and were ready to start the program in two weeks.

The following weekend the girls and I went shopping for material to make angel costumes for them to wear in a Christmas play at school. They were helpful in pinning the patterns onto the cloth and watched intently as I used the sewing machine. They looked like little angels

in the costumes with their long, blonde hair flowing under the halos. I took pictures of them to give to their friends.

The girls stayed with their mom for the Christmas holidays and I went to Detroit to visit my mother, and to attend a cousin's wedding. It was fun being with friends and relatives. Yes, I danced with every short man at the wedding.

In mid-January, Dad took his girlfriend to Cancun for a week and didn't call us. Later, when I asked him why he didn't call, he said, "I knew you could take care of everything." I said, "The point is: the girls missed you and cried because you didn't call them." I wanted to make him feel guilty so he would call them on his out-of-town trips. The girls were usually happy and outgoing, but at times, a little insecure about their family situation.

A few days later, Dad was teaching the girls a new dance step; I assumed he had learned it in Cancun with his girlfriend who was half his age. So much for immaturity.

The girls' beautiful blond hair needed special care and styling. Their hair was too long to wash in the bathroom sink, so I shampooed them as they leaned over the laundry tub. One day as eleven-year old Helen was hanging her fourteen-inch locks in the laundry tub she said: "In our anatomy class at school the teacher showed us how the female body grows a baby from an egg; but what makes that egg start to grow?"

I answered: "You know that the male has a penis ..."

"Yes, but I'm talking about the female."

"Just listen—believe me there is a connection. When the male inserts the penis into the female's vagina, he deposits sperm which unites with the egg, and that starts the growth of a baby."

She quickly raised her head up, splashing suds in my face, and with her arms akimbo, loudly said, "When I ask you a question you're supposed to tell me the truth."

I was taken aback, but managed to stifle the laughter that welled up within me as I explained the process of impregnation. With squinted eyes, she gave me a doubtful look, wrapped a towel around her head and went to her room.

In February, Anne and I became deeply involved with the students in explaining to them the Edgar Cayce legacy, and teaching them to interpret their own dreams.

America's most documented psychic, Edgar Cayce, and his associates founded the A.R.E. in 1931. The association's purpose is to research and make available information from Cayce's readings on many topics such as holistic health, vocational guidance, ESP, dreams, meditation, and to promote spiritual growth through study group meetings. As an open membership research organization, the association continues to publish such information and to sponsor conferences, seminars and lectures. (For more information go to EdgarCayce.org.)

Our dream study class of twenty-five women and five men was an intense six-week study for all of us. In addition to a two-hour class every Saturday morning, the students had several hours of homework each week remembering and analyzing their dreams so we could discuss them in class. Each student used a copy of *Following My Dreams with the Edgar Cayce Readings*, which I wrote, step-by-step for beginners in dream study. Over twenty years after publication, the A.R.E. library has six copies which are being checked out continually. It's still selling on Amazon.com, and used copies are available on Google at Rachel Kendal + dreams.

Upon completion of our studies we celebrated our accomplishments at the local pizzaria—and then exhaled. We had become friends through discussing our dreams and helping each other understand dream symbols. We kept in touch, calling each other when we needed help with interpreting our dreams.

In April I put away my books and concentrated on springtime. The daffodils and forsythia were blooming all over the neighborhood and the girls and I wanted to plant some colorful flowers in our yard—hopefully out of Shady's reach. We went to the nursery and they chose red salvia to go between the low evergreens in front of the house. My choice was black-eyed Susan to go in a large planter on the deck. Dad unloaded two large bags of top soil from the car and we started planting. Dad cleaned the grill and offered to cook burgers for dinner. We had a great time.

The girls stayed with their mom for a week during spring break from school and I went to Detroit; helped my mom in her garden and supervised cleaning and repairs in her house. When everyone returned home we made plans for the summer when the girls would be out of school. They wanted to go to a nearby camp for two weeks so we filled out the applications and got booster shots. They had matured considerably during the seven months I'd been with them. Dad and Mom had stopped fighting and Mom was allowed into the house when she picked up the girls. The divorce and property settlement were over and they stopped seeing the psychologists. Mom had a very rich boyfriend who raised horses in Leesburg, VA and Dad was still dating girls half his age. Everybody seemed to be content—again I exhaled.

While the girls were at school, I went to an ophthalmologist for an eye examination and a prescription for new glasses. As I was driving home down a two-lane road, my vision became blurred. I slowed down and the driver behind me honked his horn. So I pulled off the road onto the shoulder. As the car passed me the driver yelled, "Get off the road, you drunk." That really hurt my feelings because I was a teetotaler. I sat there for a half hour until my vision cleared. The next time I went to the ophthalmologist my friend drove me. As I think about this incident now, I laugh; but I was very upset at the time that it happened.

When school was out in June, Mom took the girls to her boyfriend's horse farm in Leesburg, VA for three weeks. They learned to ride and groom horses. It was a great experience for them. Mom was planning to get married that summer and the girls needed to get acquainted with a new stepdad. Dad was furious and bad-mouthed Mom to me. I told him to talk to his psychologist because the girls would be hurt if they saw his animosity. He really loved his girls and wanted to be a good dad, and after one session with the psychologist he understood that he had to control his anger and change his attitude toward Mom to have a peaceful family life.

It was a beautiful day and I had plenty of time off work, so Anne and I went to DC to shop for summer clothes. We went to several stores and then had lunch. As we came out of the restaurant there was a loud parade going down the street. We stood on the curb and watched as the Shriners, in their clown suits and fezzes, put on a great show for the sidewalk onlookers. The marching bands played patriotic songs from WWII. Following them were numerous acrobatic clowns and big men in little cars playfully threatening to run over our toes which were hanging over the curb. Motorcycles and fire engines roared by. Drum rolls were earsplitting, backed up by ten trumpet players who were being harassed by clowns. A 50-foot-long dragon slithered by bellowing black smoke from its nostrils, followed by twenty pipers in a row who were much quieter than the trumpet players.

I was surprised to hear Gene Autry singing *I'm Back in the Saddle Again* as three cowboys rode by us, tipping their hats and waving. Other cowboys were lassoing each other and running around shaking hands in the crowd. One of the cowboys shook my hand and said, "You sure are a pretty lady, ma'am." I laughed, thinking it was part of his act. As the crowd was dispersing, we got my car from the parking garage and headed toward home. We were on I-270 north of DC when I saw the light of a police car flashing in my rearview mirror. I looked closer and saw two men wearing cowboy hats in the front seat. I said to Anne, "I can't believe this. Two cowboys from the parade are following us in a police car!" She said, "Get in the next lane and step on it." I changed lanes and they followed me with a loud siren and more flashing lights. Other drivers were moving to the shoulder and gawking at us. As I was going 70 mph, I said, "These guys must be crazy! Shriners are respected people. They don't chase women on the interstate." Suddenly I heard an authoritative voice from a megaphone say, "Pontiac Firebird, pull over." I knew he meant me because I'd been driving a Pontiac Firebird for two years. I pulled over amid flashing lights, a loud siren and about fifty cars passing by slowly, the drivers watching me. As the "cowboy" walked toward my car I could plainly see his police uniform and I knew I was in big trouble. Anne sat beside me in shock. The officer took my driver's license back to his car, and then returned it five minutes later. He said, "Did you see my flashing lights about two miles back?"

"Yes."

"Did you hear the siren?"

"Yes."

"Why didn't you pull over?"

"I thought you were cowboys from the parade chasing us."

He looked at me, took off his hat, scratched his head and motioned for the other officer to come to my car. He squinted his eyes at me, pointed to his partner and said, "Tell him what you just told me."

"I thought you were cowboys from the parade chasing us."

They looked at each other, then looked at me, shook their heads and walked back to the police car. I drove away slowly, wondering if they were going to chase me again. As I glanced in the rearview mirror, I saw one of them seated inside the police car and the other standing beside it, holding his hat and scratching his head.

I took Anne home, and then went home and straight to bed. I was exhausted.

I visited my mother in Detroit for two weeks and helped her in the garden. She grew beautiful flowers and delicious vegetables. The weather was perfect and I got a suntan. Mother was deeply tanned and looked much younger than her seventy-five years. She was 5-feet-2-inches tall and weighed 120 pounds with only a few strands of gray hair in the dark braid that hung down her back. She was known as a feisty widow with a sharp tongue that often lashed out at the old neighborhood widowers who tried to be friendly with her. There was a five-foot chain-link fence around her property with a padlock on the gate, and she kept the key in her jeans pocket. Several times I climbed the fence to get in because she wasn't in sight when I came home. All of her women friends were avid gardeners and they talked about their plants continuously when they weren't criticizing the old widowers who kept trying to date them. One day a lucky old man was invited to sit on the patio with them to talk about flowers. After a half hour he got bored and said he had to go to a doctor's appointment. Mother and I walked him to the gate. He looked at Mother and said, "I've got two tickets for a Bob-Lo Boat cruise, would you go with me?" Mother said, "I've told you a dozen times I wouldn't go anywhere with you." He looked at me and said, "Would you go with me?" I replied, "Not a chance." We escorted him through the gate. I felt sorry for him, but not sorry enough to go out with him.

I got the names of some nearby A.R.E. members from Headquarters in Virginia Beach and attended four A.R.E. meetings while I was in Detroit. Mostly we talked about our relationship with God and our relationships with one another. I met two psychics who gave me brief readings. If you get a chance for a reading from a psychic who reads the Akashic Records, go for it. There really is a record of everything we have done, or even thought of doing. (See *Edgar Cayce on the Akashic Records* by Kevin J. Todeschi, available from A.R.E. Bookstore, 1-800-333-4499.)

I returned to Potomac and called the cleaning crew to help me get the house and yard in order for summer living. Winter clothing was stored away, slip covers put on the sofa and chairs, the carpet was cleaned; and Shady stayed for two days at the vet's getting a health checkup and doggie grooming. I stained the redwood deck furniture and we were ready to cook and eat outdoors.

The girls came home with many stories about their horse farm activities. At dinner, as they happily related their experiences with horses, I scrutinized Dad and detected that his self-control was about to slip. I gave him a blank stare and he managed to control his anger until the girls went to bed. Then he told me what he thought of their future stepdad. He said the stepdad was brainwashing the girls, among many other unkind remarks. I told him to call his psychologist, which he did the next day.

The following week I told Dad I would be leaving after the girls were settled back in school because I wanted to live in DC to be near friends and more activities. I talked to three nanny employment agencies and was assured that many jobs were available in DC. After discussing a few openings, I decided to interview with a family in northwest DC. The parents were lawyers, and Dad was a high-profile government official with an office in the Capitol in DC. Mom's office was downtown on Eye Street. I went to their home to meet Mom and six-year-old Jay. Dad wanted to see me in his office. That was my first trip to the Capitol and I thought of our forefathers and the many important people who had walked up those steps to administer to our country. As an early American history buff, during the next five years while living in DC, I enjoyed seeing the places I'd previously read about.

Dad questioned me about my credentials and warned me that my job wouldn't be easy. He was so right! I stayed with them for one year, then left to take a less demanding job. I liked the family and their friends; but there was so much activity in the household that I was usually in a state of exhaustion.

During the summer the girls went swimming several times a week, learned to cook on the grill, took care of Shady, rode bikes, and had pajama parties. They continued to spend every other weekend with Mom and went to Dad's parents in Philadelphia for the week before school started. I reminded Dad that I would be leaving in

October, and that he needed to hire someone to take my place. He protested my departure, offered me a large raise in salary, cried, and said he couldn't find anyone that could do my job. I reminded him that I had given him four months notice, and I didn't want to hear his problems. Of course, the real issue was that he didn't want the extra responsibility of caring for the girls, the house, and helping another nanny get acclimated to his lifestyle. When he understood that I was definitely leaving, he quickly found a competent woman who had raised a family of her own and she stayed with us for a week before I left. I knew that she could handle the household and I left amid kisses and tears, promising to keep in touch.

I went to Virginia Beach to unwind before starting my new job. I attended lectures at Headquarters, spent time with friends and walked on the beach for a week. The four-hour drive home gave me time to think about my new job. I was concerned about the busyness of their home and hoping Jay would get enough time with his parents. The household was totally different from the one I had just left. The dynamics within the family, and my interaction with each of them meant that I would have to change my attitude and adapt to their lifestyle. I knew I could do it and I was determined to succeed.

Re: Recommendation on behalf of Rachel Kendal
To Whom It May Concern:

Rachel Kendal has been employed by me as a live-in governess and housekeeper since September, 1982. Mrs. Kendal has been responsible for the care of my two daughters, ages 12 and 9, and the performance of all related household tasks. I am a divorced lawyer.

Mrs. Kendal's care of my daughters has been outstanding. She has always treated them with warmth and loving care. She explains reasons rather than giving orders and, thereby, quickly gained the girls' respect and trust. She has always been honest and fair with them, has kept all promises to them, and has gone far beyond the boundaries of her job title to make sure the girls were happy. She has taken them on outings, accompanied their classes to school events, and has provided a warm home environment where friends have been welcomed. Mrs. Kendal announced her intention to depart four months prior to her departure date which has given the girls ample time to adjust to her leaving and for them to understand that they were not the reason she chose to leave. Their relationship remains a warm and close one.

In summary, I recommend Mrs. Kendal without reservation as an excellent governess and home manager.

If I can answer any questions please do not hesitate to contact me at home or at work.

Sincerely,
Dad in Potomac

ADVENTURES OF A NANNY

CHAPTER 3

My new apartment was similar to the one I had just left in Rockville. The maid helped me carry in my clothes and books. The previous nanny had been there nine months and left without giving notice. The maid had been taking care of Jay and now he was my little six-year-old charge. He was a beautiful child, in good health with blue eyes and blonde curls. I looked forward to becoming his friend. He was slightly apprehensive about me taking his previous nanny's place; however, after the first week we were great friends.

The second week Mom was on a business trip and Dad came home around midnight every night. I slept upstairs in a bedroom next to Jay's so he wouldn't be alone. In the bathroom connecting the two bedrooms we could see each other in the reflection of a large mirror on the door. During the following year I spent more time in that sleeping arrangement than in my apartment. Jay's parents seldom came home before his bedtime and he needed me near him. He followed me as I went through the household chores and talked incessantly about his escapades at school. He attended a nearby school and I became a "teacher's helper" by volunteering in the classroom or school office. I loved being with the first graders, watching their excitement at learning. For their Thanksgiving party, Jay and I baked chocolate cupcakes and decorated them with orange and brown frosting.

One of Jay's classmates, Judd, lived next door and his nanny, Mary, and I took turns driving the boys to school. Mary was from Ireland, thirty years old and very pretty with long red hair and freckles across her nose. She was formerly a first grade teacher and loved children. The four of us spent a lot of time together. We went swimming, roller skating, biking, bowling and to the movies. Mary and I were back-ups for each other and got along fine. The boys were in school from 9 a.m. to 4 p.m. and I managed to tidy the kitchen, do light laundry, answer the phone, sort mail, instruct the maid who came every other day, arrange for home repairs, feed two dogs, shop for groceries and clothes for Jay and usually take a break in the afternoon to read for an hour. After 4 p.m., Jay and I had a snack and played outside. We did school work, had dinner, a bath, and read for a half hour at bedtime which was at 8 p.m.

His parents saw him briefly three evenings weekly but didn't put him to bed. My day extended to 9 p.m. almost every evening. Jay had a nanny since birth and Mom had never bathed or fed him, nor bought his clothes; she simply didn't know anything about childcare. I pitied her because she had never bonded with her child.

However, she was content in her own world and I loved to spend time with Jay. Jay had the same nanny for his first five years since birth who was an experienced mom of three kids who were now adults. I congratulated her for the good job she had done with Jay. He was highly intelligent, had good manners, and was compassionate with others and a wonderful boy.

Dad, Jay, and I flew to Los Angeles to spend the Christmas holidays with Dad's family. About two hours into the flight Jay fell asleep and Dad started talking about his lack of time with Jay. We made plans for Dad to be with Jay for two hours each Saturday and Sunday morning. On Saturdays they would be involved in sports. On Sundays they would go out for breakfast and read the comics together. I'm happy to say that Dad kept this schedule except when he was out of the country for two weeks. I usually heard them laughing on Sunday mornings and knew they were bonding and building good memories.

Dad's sister picked us up at the airport and we went home to see the rest of the family. They were lawyers, teachers, an actress and a movie producer; all in a happy mood. The next day the movie producer and actress drove Jay and me around town pointing out many famous places including the big HOLLYWOOD sign on a hillside. We went inside the studio where they were working on a movie and walked until Jay said he was tired. We drove down Rodeo Drive and saw beautifully dressed people, then had dinner at a restaurant with the entertainers singing Christmas carols. It was Christmas Eve.

The next morning at 6 a.m. Jay and I were startled to hear Santa Claus in our room saying "Ho! Ho! Ho!, it's time to wake up." Of course, it was the movie producer inside the Santa Claus suit and Jay recognized his voice. Jay jumped out of bed and ran to the Christmas tree to find his presents. Everyone was awake drinking coffee and watching Jay open his gifts. We had a great day with neighbors, cooking and eating indoors and outdoors. Jay swam with the neighbor's kids while his grandparents sat by the pool and watched them. We ate, drank and laughed in excess and I was glad to fall asleep with Jay at 9 p.m.

I woke up with an eye infection the next morning and Dad's sister took me to a clinic where I got antibiotics. I felt fine and we left for a drive up the coast to spend three days sightseeing. The first night of our trip Jay and I shared a room at a nice hotel. However, the next morning I didn't feel well enough to travel. We decided I would stay at the hotel with room service and wait for them to pick me up in two days. I must say, I thoroughly enjoyed those two days of rest. I ordered delicious meals and stayed in bed watching television, wearing sunglasses to rest my eyes.

After we returned to Los Angeles, I packed for the trip home, hugged everybody goodbye, and we got an early flight for DC where the dog sitter greeted us with complaints about the unruly dogs the minute we got in the house. I understood her complaints. The dogs were old, slept most of the time in the den, and wouldn't obey anybody. They were Dad's pets before Jay was born but there was no playful contact between them now. They were medium sized dogs of mixed breed that Dad had found abandoned on the street. When they managed to escape by climbing over a chain-link fence, the neighbors called me. So far they hadn't done any damage except to poop on a neighbor's porch. He put it into a bag and placed it by our front door. I told Mom about it and she said, "Oh, our dogs wouldn't do that."

By mid-January, Jay and I were back into the school routine and life was running smoothly for us. We had time to pursue indoor sports with Mary and Judd. The boys were on a swim team and Mary and I would drop them off at the recreation center and go for coffee and gossip with the other nannies.

Nannies met each other when we had playdates and various activities with other kids from school. Most of the nannies signed a one-year contract and left at the end of the year, usually taking another job nearby which offered a larger salary and fewer working hours. A twelve-hour day was normal for a nanny because parents either worked late or went out to dinner. We paced ourselves, hoping to avoid burnout. Families with more than two children had two nannies. When I wanted to go out in the evening and Jay's parents weren't home, I called the student nurses' dormitory at Georgetown University and got a very capable babysitter. We lived about two miles from the University, and it was convenient for the students to do their homework after Jay went to bed. He liked the nurses and felt secure with them. It was a good arrangement for all of us. For Easter vacation, Mom, Dad and Jay made plans to meet Dad's parents at Martha's Vineyard in Massachusetts, and I planned to go to New Mexico with three other nannies. Before we left we went to see the cherry blossoms at the Tidal Basin in DC. Standing there surrounded by the beautiful pink blossoms, I explained to the boys that the cherry trees were a gift to the American people from Japan in 1912. Jay said, "Aren't they the guys who bombed Pearl Harbor?" I replied, "Yes, but we're friends now."

Mary and I, with two other nannies, flew to Albuquerque, NM and rented a car at the airport. We had reservations at a nearby hotel for two nights. The next day we visited the Albuquerque Balloon Museum because we wanted to go skyward if possible. The guide said nearly 750 hot-air balloons participate every year in the Hot-Air Balloon Fiesta. However, it wasn't fiesta time and the weather wasn't suitable for a flight that day; but we learned about balloons and decided we would go up sometime soon.

We had dinner and went to check out the evening activities. Bright lights, music, and dancing in the street seemed to be the norm. We joined in and danced until midnight.

The next morning we drove about an hour to Santa Fe and reserved hotel rooms for two nights so we could enjoy the local culture. The Santa Fe Trail started to bring Americans across the prairie and into northern New Mexico back in 1821. Spain was running things then, having wrested control away from the Pueblo Indians who had settled it centuries before. Those same Spaniards built the Palace of the Governors in 1610 in the center of town, now the oldest continuously operated public building in America. Inside, the low-slung adobe is full of colonial and territorial history. Outside, the sidewalks bustle with Native American artists and jewelry makers—the only group allowed to set up shop on this part of the plaza. The American Planning Association recently named this narrow winding street, lined with many eateries as one of the country's best. A great walking opportunity if you've got sensible shoes!

We were prepared for walking with a guide that we hired for four hours to tour the city with us. We went to the Institute of America Indian Arts Museum, the Georgia O'Keefe Museum and the Children's Museum. I was glad to learn that in the 1950s legislation was passed requiring all new buildings to be done in Pueblo Revival and Territorial architectural styles. No tall tower or grandiose statements in steel or glass. Even the capital building keeps a low adobe style profile. And that truly makes the city special. (The santafesite.com is a great resource for learning more about the town as well as its arts and cultural opportunities.) After dinner we joined the revelers for singing and dancing.

We got up early the next morning and had a delicious breakfast. I had Eggs Ole' which consisted of baked eggs with a savory southwest flavor including tomatoes, corn, black olives, cilantro, green chilies and Mexican cheese with a side order of breakfast potatoes. I was glad to be wearing stretch pants. My waistline increased two inches during breakfast.

We drove about sixty-five miles north of Santa Fe to visit Taos Pueblo. We were fascinated with its world-famous multi-storied adobe architecture which is one of North America's oldest continuously occupied villages and a World Heritage Site and National Historic Site. Taos, NM is an art mecca with over 100 galleries and museums featuring works of art by such notables as R.C. Gorman, Amado Pena and Georgia O'Keefe. We bought beautifully handmade silver and turquoise jewelry. I couldn't resist buying an Indian blanket which I wrapped up in many times while watching television with Jay.

At the Taos Plaza we munched on delicious Indian bread which was baked in the traditional earthen ovens and drank cold, locally made root beer from one of the vendors. We sat on benches and relaxed, enjoying the blue sky, sunshine and the magic of Taos.

We drove back to our hotel in Albuquerque late that evening and prepared for a morning flight the next day back to DC.

The dog sitter greeted me with a grouchy attitude and I knew I'd have to find a person who liked dogs for my next trip. She knew what the job entailed so why did she keep coming back if she didn't like it? I didn't call her again.

I got up early Sunday morning and went to the Georgetown Safeway about 10 a.m. to get fresh food for the family. I was looking at berries when I heard a male voice say, "Those are nice strawberries." I looked up to see a handsome man about thirty years old with a big smile on his face. I smiled and said, "Yes, they are." As I walked down the aisles of food, three more men with big smiles made comments to me about the food. I thought that was strange because Safeway shoppers usually focus on whatever they want to buy, not on making comments to other shoppers. Later that day I told Mary about my morning shopping trip and she laughed uproariously. She said, "Didn't you know that the Safeway is a "Meet Market" on Sunday mornings? I said, "What does that mean?" She said, "Single people go there to find a date." I was dumbfounded. I would no longer be shopping there on Sunday mornings.

On a nice sunny day, Mary and I took the boys to Arlington National Cemetery. They listened intently as the guide explained the history of the cemetery. We watched the preparations for a burial and the ritual of the changing of the Honor Guard. We were in awe as jets flew overhead and the rifles were fired in tribute to a fallen war hero. We went to the grave of President John F. Kennedy and I explained to them the assassination, and how it saddened everyone. As we watched the Eternal Flame flicker, I felt tears run down my cheek; I remembered that fateful day of November 22, 1963. This afternoon had been an introduction to patriotism, war, death and reverence to two six-year-old boys. On the way home they asked many questions about the ceremonies we had witnessed. The day had been a solemn experience for all of us.

Dad invited us to have dinner at the Capitol with senators and other high-ranking officials, and of course I wanted to go so I could gawk at everyone. We rode the little Senate trolley in the Capitol basement which reminded me of the kids' amusement park. The women wore beautiful dresses and jewelry. The men were neat in their dark suits. The children were well-dressed and well-mannered because several nannies were present to keep them under control while their parents socialized. The atmosphere was friendly and fun and I met several people whose pictures I had seen in the newspaper.

The next day I got a call from a retired official asking me to go to lunch with him at a restaurant two days later. When I arrived, he was waiting in the lobby and we were seated immediately. He seemed a little nervous but I didn't get my guard up until he started talking about how lonely he was. He was sixty-five years old, had been a widower for four years and wanted more excitement in his life. We were halfway through the meal when he asked me to be his weekend girlfriend for a sleepover at this house. For three seconds I considered slapping his face and pouring a cup of coffee on his head, but I burst into maniacal laughter and walked out. So much for senile old men.

Mom and Dad took Jay to Williamsburg, VA for Memorial Day weekend, and Mary and I went on a day-trip to Leesburg, VA to go up in a hot-air balloon. On Saturday we drove West on Route 7. It started to rain and we were hoping the weather would clear up before launch time. About a hundred people milled around inspecting the balloons and listening to the bad weather reports. We were again disappointed as we drove back home. I told Mary, "Someday we'll make it." The next day we went shopping in Georgetown, ate at Hamburger Hamlet, then watched *Gone With the Wind* on television that evening. That weekend was a nice break from our weekly routine with the boys.

We studied the brochures for boys' summer camps and found one that everyone agreed would be fun. Jay and Judd chose a ranch in Manassas, VA where they could ride horses and sleep in a bunkhouse. They would learn to feed dogs, cats, chickens, rabbits and goats, and cook over a camp fire. Swimming in a creek, bike riding, baseball and hiking in the hills would keep them busy during the afternoons. After dinner they could roast marshmallows and sing around the camp fire. We made reservations for the last week of June.

I decided to stay home the week the boys were at camp and supervise some painters in painting three rooms on the main floor of the house. I discussed my plans with Mom and Dad and they agreed the rooms needed to be painted. I called a painting company, a man came and checked the three rooms, gave me an estimate of the cost, and said that the painters would start at 8 a.m. the following Monday morning.

Three painters were there at 8 a.m. and each one of them picked the room they wanted to work in. They went out to lunch at noon and I checked the rooms. They hadn't opened a can of paint. For four hours that morning they had been preparing to paint by taping around woodwork and windows, moving furniture, and spreading drop cloths over the carpet. Apparently they had been moving in slow-motion. They didn't come back after lunch. They were there with smiles the next morning at 8 a.m. I didn't smile. They went to their rooms and I ignored them. I was hoping they would work faster because I had to stay in the house while they were there. If they had told me they weren't coming back the previous afternoon I could have run errands; instead I had to shop in the evening, which I didn't like to do. At noon when they told me they were going to lunch I asked them if they would be back that day. They explained to me that they worked at another house nearby in the afternoon so they could do two jobs in one week. I was furious because I knew they couldn't finish our house in a week and I was stuck in my schedule while trying to work around them.

Mom and Dad had gone to New York City for a few days and since I was housebound, I hired a reliable cleaning company who sent two strong men and a capable woman to help me attack every bit of dust in the house. On all three levels, the house sparkled in two days—

except for the three rooms that were being painted. On Thursday morning I offered the painters a deal and they accepted. I agreed to make their lunch on Thursday and Friday if they would stay and work from 8 a.m. to 6 p.m. and finish the job. Also, if they completely finished on Friday, I would give each of them a fifty-dollar bonus. They agreed and got busy. Thursday's lunch was chili with shredded cheese, cornbread, coleslaw, with fruit and cookies for dessert, and lots of black coffee. They gobbled it up, took a ten-minute break and smoked on the deck. I gave them my approval at the end of the day. Friday's lunch was foot-long submarine sandwiches, mixed veggies, chocolate pudding and more black coffee, which they drank during the rest of the day. At 6 p.m. I inspected the rooms and congratulated them on a job well done. They each got a fifty-dollar bill and we were all happy.

Jay and Judd told us about their adventures at camp. They had a great time. They looked a little grungy with sunburns, and Band-Aids on their legs, but they were back to normal in a couple of days. Mary and I took them shopping to buy clothes for summer. They enjoyed picking out their own clothes and trying them on. After lunch we went to see *Bambi* which is one of my favorite kids' movies. That evening Dad asked me to pack for Jay to spend a week in Los Angeles with him and his family.

Mom would be in Phoenix on a business trip, and I would have free time to visit my mother in Detroit.

While I was in Detroit I called Edgar Cayce's Association for Research and Enlightenment, Inc. (A.R.E.) to get the name and phone number of any A.R.E. members nearby. Sylvia lived only a mile from my mother and she picked me up that evening to attend a meeting at her house. Six members were present and we discussed the *Search for God* book which contains advice on how to live a happy spiritual life. I felt refreshed after spending an evening with like-minded people. There are approximately thirty thousand A.R.E. members worldwide; most of them are within the United States. (See Edgar Cayce.org)

The next day four of us went to Toledo, OH (about an hour's drive) to attend an A.R.E. seminar pertaining to the fundamental concepts of the energy system of the human body. Every cell in the human body vibrates with energy. This fact, long understood by traditional cultures around the world, is confirmed by many of today's scientific advances and discoveries—we do consist of more than just the muscles, bones, and blood of our physical bodies. The human aura—a colored halo or force field surrounding the body—can be used, among other things, to assess your health or gain a greater awareness of yourself and others. (See *Edgar Cayce on the Aura*)

My mom and I worked in her garden which fascinated me with the many beautiful flowers, and especially the day lilies with their variety of colors. She had been a gardener since childhood when she learned from her mother how to grow and can vegetables. It's hard work, but at eighty years old she could easily bend over and hoe, with her long braid swinging down her back. She no longer canned vegetables, as we easily consumed and gave to the neighbors the carrots, broccoli, Swiss chard, leaf lettuce, cabbage and beets that grew abundantly under her attentive care. Every morning she was up at 5 a.m. and sat at the kitchen table drinking coffee, waiting for daylight so she could go work in her garden. The day before I left to return to DC, we sat in the shade of a maple tree, had lunch and gossiped with the neighbors while a housekeeping crew put the house in order.

Jay and Judd were happy to have time together. They spent many hours during the summer in a pile of wet sand in our backyard building "cities." They stayed outdoors most of the time riding bikes, roller skating and exploring in the park. Of course, either Mary or I had them in sight as they went about their activities. We were always alert to keep them from harm. One day, when the dog groomer pulled his van into the driveway to bathe the dogs, the boys wanted to watch him. I stood in the doorway of the van and watched everybody. I'd read about many cases of kidnapped children and I never let my guard down.

The first weekend in August Mom and Dad took Jay to New York City to see a Broadway play in which a friend of theirs was playing the leading role. They had lunch in the Rainbow Room at Rockefeller Center and visited the Statue of Liberty. Jay was impressed and told me every detail about his weekend. I stayed home that weekend, relaxed and watched movies on television. However, I was a bit apprehensive because I knew it would be easy for a burglar to break into the house. There was no burglar alarm system, and the dogs wouldn't hear any intrusion because they were nearly deaf. I locked all the doors and stayed in my room until daylight.

The boys went to camp in mid-August. They were going to learn to be little gentlemen—we hoped. The camp was located in Middleburg, VA about an hour's drive from home, in a large estate that had everything for living luxuriously on forty acres of beautiful surroundings. Mom and Dad spent an afternoon there with the camp director and the parents of the other boys who would be there for a week of learning and fun.

Mary and I went to Virginia Beach for five days of swimming, sun bathing and socializing with some of my old friends at A.R.E. Mary was intrigued by the many activities at Headquarters. We joined others at noon each day in the meditation room, spent several hours in the library, and attended a lecture every evening.

One day, while we were meditating in a group, I heard the rustling of paper nearby but tried to ignore it. Within a few seconds I heard a loud voice say, "Let me go." I opened my eyes to see the meditation leader grasping a teenage boy by his arm. Other men moved in to subdue him. Both the boy's hands were full of dollar bills that he had taken from the donations basket while our eyes were closed. This was a sad situation; as we found out later, the boy was a runaway from New York, and after a call to his parents, was put on a bus to go back home. Other than that incident we enjoyed our trip and reviewed the lectures on our four-hour drive back home.

Jay and Judd talked incessantly about their camp activities. I could see that their table manners had improved. They sat up straight, used the proper fork and didn't talk with their mouths full. They combed their hair and dressed nearly every morning; then tidied their rooms. I was hoping this behavior would last. In addition to sports: swimming, golf and soccer, they had gone bird-watching in the woods, and learned to identify trees by the shape of their leaves. They attended a symphony and talked to the musicians about the instruments. There were books and movies for afternoon rest periods. They wrote in a journal at bedtime, but Jay refused to let me read his. We considered the week in Middleburg a well-rounded program for a boy Jay's age.

No one in our house attended church so I consulted with Mom and Dad about religious training for Jay. The agreed for him to start religion classes after school in September. I bought a Children's Bible and as he read it we discussed the life of Jesus. He was very attentive and asked serious questions. Mary made arrangements for Judd to attend the same class with Jay at a nearby church.

School started after Labor Day and we settled into our routine. In mid-September, the nanny agency called to remind me that my one-year contract would soon expire, and she had a better job for me. I listened as she told me about the family: two boys, ages two and five, Mom was a dentist, Dad was an ophthalmologist, their offices were in DC, my working hours would be 9 a.m. to 5:30 p.m. with no weekend hours, a small apartment, and they were paying fifty dollars more per week than my present salary. The family's previous nanny had a health problem, and a temporary nanny would be there until they could find a permanent one. It sounded interesting and I offered to interview with them.

After meeting the boys and the parents, I agreed to take the job as soon as my present employers found a replacement for me. Within two weeks, my agency found someone for them, and I moved about a mile away to start another episode in my life: another home, another job and two little strangers. I promised Jay to keep in touch. He had grown to be quite self-sufficient at taking care of himself during the year I was with him, and I felt that my new little charges needed me more than he did. Actually, I had spent more time supervising maids and repairmen, caring for dogs, answering phones and processing mail, grocery shopping and planning dinner parties, and being on call seven days a week than I had spent with Jay. It was written into my contract that I would work up to sixty hours per week; but I stayed with Jay on weekends when no babysitter was available. I wanted my evenings and weekends free so I could pursue some classes at Georgetown University, and socialize with friends. Mary and I set a date to take Jay and Judd out to lunch and a movie for the following weekend and I moved to my new environment.

October 11, 1984

To Whom It May Concern

The purpose of this letter is to recommend Rachel Kendal for any position of responsibility which would require a competent, reliable and pleasant employee.

Rachel worked for my wife and me for approximately one year, helping us with the care of our son and the management of our household. During that period, she supervised our move to our present address and oversaw the remodel work of the basement into a small apartment. At all times and with all tasks she was totally reliable and extremely capable. She is very pleasant to deal with.

My wife and I offer our strongest recommendation of her character and ability and will be pleased to respond to inquiries regarding her employment.

Jay's Dad

ADVENTURES OF A NANNY

CHAPTER 4

On the next job, I adored the boys, and after observing them for a week, I realized that two-year-old Zack and four-year-old Josh needed some self-discipline. There was too much punching and crying going on. Mom and Dad had breakfast with the boys every morning, then left for work at 9 a.m. I took over, helping them to get dressed and tidy their rooms. While they watched cartoons on TV, I tidied the kitchen and started one load of laundry. We played outside until lunchtime. I drove Josh to his preschool at 1 p.m. and picked him up at 4 p.m. During the afternoon Zack took a two-hour nap and I read or watched a movie on TV. There were no pets in the household, which was a big relief for me.

The maid came twice weekly to clean and do laundry, and she was very efficient without any supervision. I had time to devise a procedure to eliminate the sibling rivalry. Josh was the instigator of the punching and crying, so I monitored his behavior, hoping to avoid trouble. He wanted my undivided attention and often punched Zack when I was caring for him. Dad told me that Josh's preschool teacher considered him mentally and emotionally handicapped because he caused so many interruptions in class. I told Dad I would observe Josh before I formed an opinion about his mentality.

The next morning while the boys were watching TV, Josh hit Zack on the head with his fist. Zack started crying and Josh ran upstairs. I ran after him and saw him crawl under his bed. I lay down on the floor, reached under the bed, grabbed his leg and pulled him out—not too gently. I picked him up and sat him on his bed, grasped him by the back of the neck, and looking into his eyes firmly, said, "You will not hit your brother!" He glared at me with his eyes wide open. He was terrified. He got the message, and he didn't like it. I told him to apologize to Zack—which he did reluctantly. We went outside to play and several times he glanced at me as he kicked the ball around the yard. Miraculously, he never hit Zack again, and I never mentioned the incident to anyone. For two years in a Detroit Headstart Program I had dealt with tough little boys. They needed to know who was in charge.

The three of us cuddled up in a big chair with me in the middle, and read two or three times a day. We used picture books with large print, and Josh learned to recite the alphabet within a month. Both boys could identify words on flash cards. We had fun learning. After a couple of months working with books and flash cards, I was stunned one day to see Josh reading to Zack. When I told their parents that evening that Josh could read, they wanted to hear him immediately. His mom cried with joy. He was not mentally handicapped as the teacher had suggested. In fact, he was exceptionally bright to be reading at age four. We knew he needed to be in a different preschool.

Josh thrived in his morning class at the new school. Mom drove him to school each morning on her way to work and I picked him up at 1 p.m. He took his lunch in a lunch box that I helped him buy, and he felt like a big boy. He cooperated with his teacher, and I never got a bad report about him. When we got home from school each day, Zack took a nap and I gave Josh my undivided attention. He was a fast learner and I enjoyed teaching him.

Zack was almost three years old, and tried to emulate his big brother. He memorized the stories in the picture books and pretended to read them. He was a natural entertainer and sang a lot. His voice was extremely loud and strong for one so young, and his acting was comical in his zeal to please his audience. I taught him an old song from 1938, by Johnny Mercer and Harry Warren, titled, *You Must Have Been a Beautiful Baby*, and recorded his act on a video camera. His parents were delighted and sent the videotape to his maternal grandmother in NJ who showed it to all of her friends.

Both boys were handsome, healthy, outgoing and loved to perform for the camera. When they went to visit relatives on Christmas vacation, they took several videotapes to flaunt their talent to the captive audience in NJ. Mom and Dad were capable of caring for the boys and didn't need my help on the trip, so Mary and I went to Saint Thomas, in the Virgin Islands, to soak up some sunshine.

My friend, Melanie, had lived on Saint Thomas for five years and worked at the Chase Manhattan Bank in downtown Charlotte Amalie. When she invited me for the holidays, I was eager to go. We went to the beach the first day we were there. Mary, in a skimpy bikini, attracted the attention of several nearby males. With her long red hair and perfect body, she looked like a movie star. However, she had no interest in the oglers because she had a great boyfriend in DC. Melanie and I, both pushing forty (but healthy and attractive), definitely had no interest in the young beach boys. We simply soaked up the sunshine.

The next day the three of us went to Puerto Rico in a small plane that flew so low I could see the fish swimming in the aqua water below us. We had lunch, and took a guided tour, and shopped. At dusk we returned to Charlotte Amalie for dinner. For two more days we relaxed on the beach and got great suntans.

The novelty of picking bananas from a tree in the backyard of Melanie's home was delightful. Those little lizards that seemed to be everywhere were annoying as they stood their ground and stared at me. However, they are part of the island experience, so I just avoided them.

One day, after shopping and lunch downtown, Mary and I settled down on a park bench to watch the people go by. Everyone seemed to be in a good mood as they meandered about the beautiful tropical setting. As we sat there listening to a babbling brook, a man stopped and urinated in the water. We were stunned by this behavior and told Melanie about it as soon as we got home. She laughed and said it was acceptable on Saint Thomas, that natives were easygoing and nobody complained about such incidents. I wasn't that laid-back, but as a tourist I had no authority to set standards for the natives. Therefore, I ignored the situation, and Mary and I flew back to DC the next day.

I had become friendly with three nannies and their charges who played with Zack and Josh in a nearby park. The nannies and I chatted while watching the children play on the swings and slides. When a strange nanny with two children approached us and introduced herself, we welcomed her to our play group. They had recently moved to DC from New York City. We invited her to join our Association of DC Area Nannies (ADCAN), which met biweekly at a nearby school to discuss our interactions with the children and parents that we worked with. Beverly told us about herself: She was thirty-five years old, had a bachelor's degree in social work, had been with her present family for six years. She seemed to be devoted to the four-year-old girl and five-year-old boy, but felt that her fourteen-hour work days were overwhelming because she didn't have enough time for herself. We agreed with her and made suggestions for talking about her plight with her employer. A few days later she told us that the mother of the children had agreed to care for them one afternoon a week so Beverly could explore DC.

Two days later, when I answered the doorbell, I found the children looking up at me. Their mother was in a car parked on the street, and waved to me as she drove away. I brought the children in, and called their home four times that afternoon to no avail. Apparently, their mom thought I was a free babysitter. I gave them lunch and played with all four children until the doorbell rang at five o'clock while I was preparing dinner. A very embarrassed Beverly apologized for the imposition of her employer. It was Beverly's afternoon off duty, and her employer brought the children to me for a playdate. I told her to advise her employer that if it happened again, I would call the police and report them as abandoned children. It never happened again.

Beverly's employer hired a part-time babysitter to help with the children, and she and I attended some evening art and religion classes at Georgetown University. She also shared the love of gardening with me. In the spring Mom and Dad landscaped the area surrounding the house with an exquisite array of trees, shrubs, and flowers, and prepared a plot on the back of the property for growing vegetables. Beverly and I spent many happy hours teaching the children to garden with us. They learned to cultivate and water the plants, and never refused to eat the vegetables we grew. During the summer the flowers bloomed profusely with many beautiful colors. Neighbors who were walking their dogs congratulated us; people driving by stopped to stare at the plants. We were all very proud of our accomplishments.

The last week of July the boys went to day camp in Potomac, MD. Every morning at 8 a.m. I drove them to a church parking lot in Chevy Chase, MD, where a bus picked them up. One morning as we were running across the parking lot to catch the bus, Josh pointed to a crucifix on the front of the church and said, "What is that?" I said, "That's Jesus on the cross." He said, "Why?" I couldn't answer his question at the moment, but later that evening I asked Mom if I could teach the boys some Bible stories and she said, "Keep it Jewish." I bought several cartoon videos depicting the lives of biblical characters: Moses, Joshua, Samson, Daniel, David, Solomon, and others. I told the boys the stories were about Jewish heroes. Mom and Dad approved. I enjoyed watching the videos with them and answering their many insightful questions.

Life at camp didn't go well. Most of the days they were outside with dogs and cats as they played baseball, soccer, basketball, and hiked through the woods with the temperature above 85°. They were exhausted and dirty when I picked them up at 5 p.m. I gave them a cold drink and put them in the shower. They ate dinner and fell into a stupor in front of the TV.

A few days later I noticed they were scratching their heads. I examined their hair and found lice. This was a problem Mom wouldn't like. I snipped a few hairs from each head with lice clinging to them, placed them on a piece of white paper, secured them with Scotch tape, and laid them on the kitchen windowsill. Later that evening when I told Mom the bad news, she said, "My kids don't have head lice." I referred her to the windowsill. After a few expletives, she said, "What are we going to do?" I told her I would call the doctor in the morning. I followed the doctor's orders and the problem was solved within a week.

In August, Beverly and I took the children on several day trips in the DC area. We packed a picnic basket and went to explore Rock Creek Park with binoculars. We learned the history of the Chesapeake and Ohio Canal as we rode the canal boat which was pulled by mules on the towpath. We visited the National Cathedral, the Smithsonian Museum and the White House. We also shopped for several days for school clothes. The boys were quite adept at picking out their own clothes. They found the right sizes and matched the colors perfectly.

At mealtime we discussed the nutritive value of the food we were eating, and the variety of vitamins contained in the vegetables we grew and ate. They liked to read food labels and insisted on whole grain cereal with a minimum amount of sugar. One morning as I served French toast with butter and syrup, Zak said:

"Where does French toast come from?"

"Bread and eggs."

"Where does the bread come from?"

"Flour and wheat."

"Where does the butter come from?"

"Milk and cows."

"Where does the syrup come from?"

"Sap from the maple trees."

"Where does the French come from?"

"I don't know—go get dressed."

Beverly and I went to visit my mother for the Labor Day weekend. I took her to Greenfield Village and the Henry Ford Museum in Dearborn, MI, and told her about my interests there since I was eight years old. I remember my third grade class gathered around the glass-enclosed chair that President Lincoln was sitting in when he was shot. My interest in early American history started that day; and as I grew up, got married, and raised three daughters, we frequently attended events held at the Village and Museum.

Josh started all-day kindergarten at a nearby private school, and Zack went with him every morning at 9 a.m. to attend preschool in the same building. Mom drove them to school and I picked up Zack at 1 p.m., and then we picked up Josh at 3 p.m. The boys easily adapted to the new routine and enjoyed making new friends. After school on Wednesdays Josh played soccer with his peers while Zack and I cheered them on. One day while we were sitting on a bench on the edge of the soccer field, a man sat down beside us and started observing the nearby woods with binoculars. I glanced at him and he said he wanted to be sure the kids were safe while playing near the woods. I had read in the Washington Post a warning about rabid raccoons and thought that he was referring to them. However, during a brief conversation, I learned that he was a bodyguard for one of the boys on Josh's team who was the son of a high-profile government official. I felt uncomfortable about sitting near someone carrying a gun under his jacket. The next Wednesday I sat on the bench with two moms and their toddlers. I didn't want to get involved in a situation where a child might be kidnapped amid gunfire.

For Thanksgiving vacation Mom and Dad took the boys to Disneyland, and I went to Premier, WV for a family reunion. I boarded a small, loudly vibrating plane with six passengers at Dulles Airport, and we flew over the mountains to Bluefield, WV in seventy-five minutes. My cousin, Lena, met me and we drove to Premier in forty-five minutes. The next day seventy-two relatives met at a church hall to celebrate. Their ages ranged from six weeks to ninety-seven years. We had a wonderful time feasting conversing, dancing, and shooting videos. I was born in Premier, then taken to Dearborn, MI at age four when my parents divorced. My dad's relatives were in Premier and my mother's in Dearborn. Three days later, I flew back to Dulles where Beverly picked me up for dinner.

The boys did well at school and, at home, we prepared the garden plot for winter. Time seemed to fly by. Mom, Dad, and the boys went to NJ for the Christmas holidays, and I went to visit my mother. We didn't go out much because the weather was so cold in Detroit, but we enjoyed our time together reminiscing and watching TV.

While the boys were in school I had time to get involved with several friends in studying the Edgar Cayce Readings. We met one morning a week for two hours to study the *Search for God* book which was compiled by the first study group —Norfolk 1 in Norfolk, VA. They were guided by readings from Edgar Cayce from 1931 through 1942. In essence, we were encouraging each other to live by the Golden Rule: Treat others as you wish them to treat you, love your neighbor as yourself. I believe if everyone followed this rule there would be peace on earth. The wisdom from the textbook helped us to stay on the right path. We were a close-knit group who enjoyed being together. We drove to a weekend conference in Virginia Beach while the children were on their Easter vacation break from school.

After living in DC for five years, enjoying the many learning opportunities in such a great city, I wanted a more sedate lifestyle so I could contemplate the next phase of my life. I informed Mom that I wanted to leave in three months, after summer was over, and the boys were back in school. She burst into tears, and I assured her I would stay until she found another nanny. I intended to finish the religion lessons with the boys, help them with reading, math, and geography that they had been studying at school, and plant another garden.

The family went to NJ for the last week of June and I worked in the garden. When the boys returned we started our weekly routine. After breakfast, we studied for an hour, then went outside to play and work in the garden. The boys were fascinated with the insects that were amongst the plants. They soon learned not to bother the bees, but handled the lady bugs and praying mantises with ease.

Zack no longer needed an afternoon nap so we went swimming with other children almost every afternoon in the pool where Beverly lived. We often discussed religion at their level of understanding, as we lounged around the pool. The boys were Jewish; I was Christian, and we focused on the similarities of various religions. They didn't go to camp that summer because we had so much fun: flying kites at the National Mall, eating lunch by the Chesapeake and Ohio canal locks in Georgetown, going to the top of the Washington Monument and viewing DC, and attending a Sunday service at Saint John's Church across the street from the White House on Lafayette Square—the church attended by presidents since 1816.

In July there was a burglary at the nearby embassy which necessitated protecting our neighborhood with armed mounted policemen. To reiterate: I don't like guns! I told the boys to stay away from the policemen and their horses. The policemen showed no friendliness towards us, so I avoided making eye contact with them. However, I knew they were surveying everybody and everything as their horses clippity-clopped down the street. The boys just stopped and stared at them as they went riding by. It was not a pleasant situation, but we hoped they would serve as a deterrent to any criminals stalking our neighborhood.

One afternoon when the boys and I were working in the garden, a large rabid raccoon staggered into our yard. We were frightened and ran into the house. I called 911 and within a few minutes a mounted policeman came and threw a net over it which rendered it helpless until the animal control men arrived, put it in a cage and took it away in a truck. The boys watched the proceedings in awe. We discussed the incident and they understood that they should stay away from raccoons.

One afternoon I left the boys at the pool with Beverly so I could go grocery shopping. I pulled into the store's parking lot, parked the car, got out, closed the car door, and realized I'd locked my purse and keys in the car. I knew there was another car key in my dresser drawer and I was only two blocks from home. I had set the burglar alarm before leaving home and the house key to deactivate it was on the ring with the car key, which was locked inside the car. There was only one way I could get into the house—through a small bathroom window in my basement apartment. I figured my 110 pound body could squeeze through the window. I pulled the grating off the window well and jumped down into the hole. Luckily, the window was open so I lifted it out of the frame and placed it on top of the grating which was lying on the grass. I put my feet and legs through the window so that my legs dangled into the bathroom while I was in a sitting position. I turned over onto my stomach so that my legs and buttocks were inside the window ledge as I inched my way in, figuring that my feet would touch the top of the bathtub, and I would be able to balance myself there while pulling my head and shoulders into the bathroom. I had almost made it when I heard an authoritative voice say, "Come out of there with your hands up." I knew it was the Mountie. I said, "If I put my hands up, I'll fall into the bathtub."

At that instant my feet touched the bathtub. I pulled the rest of my body inside, got out of the bathtub, ran upstairs, turned off the burglar alarm, and ran to the side of the house where the Mountie was down in the window well looking for me. He didn't look happy as I tried to explain why I was breaking and entering my own apartment. However, he did recognize me as a resident of that particular house and he believed me. He left frowning. I put the window and grating back in place, washed up, changed clothes, got the keys from the drawer, and went to buy groceries.

Beverly and I took the children to Fredricksburg, VA which is only a one-hour drive from DC. I had been there previously and was able to guide our group and explain the significance of the small town of 20,000 residents. Fredericksburg is a scene of three hundred years of early American history including George Washington's boyhood home and The President James Monroe (1817-25) Museum. Several Civil War battles were fought there in which Confederate forces were victorious. We walked the streets and visited homes of some of the patriots who formed the foundation of our country. The children, who ranged in age from six to nine years old, were in awe of the old-fashioned household furnishings and the way people lived in the past centuries. We left Fredericksburg at 8 p.m., and all of the children fell asleep on the drive home. For the next few days we reinforced what they had learned with conversations about what we had seen. They were enthusiastic with questions and comments, and I knew that they had a good introduction to early American history.

They did well in math, spelling, and reading during the summer, and I felt that their teachers would be pleased with their progress when school started in September. They knew all of the dialogue of the biblical heroes in the videos they watched. They read every day and their vocabulary was far above their grade level at school. I was proud of them, and I knew I had done a good job in helping them to get a head start in life. I had been with them for an enjoyable four years and they were ready to face the world without me. I needed a slower, quieter environment so I could attend some classes and get involved in activities with Edgar Cayce's Association for Research and Enlightenment (A.R.E.).

I became interested in the A.R.E. In 1968 after reading *There Is A River: The Story of Edgar Cayce* by Thomas Sugrue. This biography of Edgar Cayce covers not only his fascinating life and the phenomenal information that came through his psychic readings, but it also provides hope to anyone suffering from illness or despair of heart and spirit. The myriad topics covered include holistic health remedies to both common and rare illnesses; spiritual growth subjects such as meditation, prayer, and reincarnation; and world events—past, present, and future.

In 2000 *Edgar Cayce An American Prophet*, by Sidney D. Kirkpatrick was published which gives a personal account of Edgar Cayce and his work. This, and other books are available from AREPRESS.com or ARECATALOG.com.

When I lived in Virginia Beach, VA (1980-81), I attended a seminar conducted by Delores Krieger, PhD., R.N., a prominent professor of nursing at the New York University of Nursing. She demonstrated to us a method of healing called Therapeutic Touch (TT). First she directed us to rub our palms together for about twenty strokes, then separate them to four inches apart so we could feel the energy between them. This was to establish that there is an energy field emitted from our bodies. We spent several hours exploring this energy by touching each other and listening to her lecture. Everyone in the class of fifty learned to manipulate this energy. TT was initially developed for persons in the health professions, but is currently taught worldwide to anyone who is interested in learning the technique. As of 1998, an estimated 100,000 people around the world have been trained in TT; 43,000 of those persons are health care professionals, many of whom use TT in conjunction with traditional medicine, as well as osteopathic, chiropractic, naturopathic, and homeopathic therapies. TT is taught in over 100 colleges, universities, and medical schools. (See Delores Kreiger.com)

Mom had read my "dreams" book in which I wrote about this method of healing, and when she developed pneumonia she asked me to use TT on her. She had been lying in bed for two days with a fever, taking antibiotics, and said she would try anything that might help. I sat beside her on the bed, silently said The Lord's Prayer, placed my hands on her chest for one minute, then asked, "Did you feel anything?" She said, "It felt like rivulets of electricity running through my body. I breathed deeply, and I felt good." She slept for two hours, then came downstairs, ate dinner, and went to work the next morning. I have been performing this type of TT healing since 1979. I've seen many people practice TT. Almost anyone can do it with proper training.

The Divine Matrix Bridging Time, Space, Miracles, and Belief, by Gregg Braden, is a comprehensive study on how this energy works. Braden states: "Between 1993 and 2000, a series of ground-breaking experiments revealed dramatic evidence of a web of energy that connects everything in our lives and our world—the Divine Matrix. From the healing of our bodies to the success of our careers, relationships, and the peace between nations, this new evidence demonstrates that we each hold the power to speak directly to the force that links all of creation. What would it mean to discover that the power to create joy, heal suffering, and bring peace to nations lives inside of you? How differently would you live if you knew how to use this power each day of your life? You can join many others on this extraordinary journey, bridging science, spirituality, and miracles through the language of the Divine Matrix."

I called the nanny agency and learned about a newborn baby boy who would need a nanny in mid-September. I visited the family in Vienna, VA, a half-hour drive from DC, and accepted the job of taking care of him after his grandmother left in September. I babysat for him on two weekends before I moved there so his mom and dad could show his grandmother the tourist attractions in DC before she went home to Utah. I explained to Josh and Zack why I would be leaving, and they understood that they were big boys and could take care of themselves with a little help from a housekeeper when they weren't in school. I showed them pictures of baby Gary, and promised to bring him to visit them.

Through August we continued swimming, gardening, and playing outside. One evening at dusk the three of us were playing hide-and-seek and I hid behind a large shrub near my bathroom window. I sat there quietly for a few minutes waiting for Josh to come looking for me. Suddenly, I heard a loud voice say, "Come out with your hands up!" I recognized that voice. He actually had his gun pointed at the shrub in front of me! I was furious. I said, "Put the gun away—there are children nearby." He said, "Oh, it's you again." He put the gun back in the holster. Josh and Zack ran up and put their arms around me. I realized he was only doing his duty, but as we watched the Mountie ride away, I sent out thought forms that screamed: "I hope I never see you again, Mr. Hop-a-long. Hi-Ho Silver to you—and good riddance!"

October 4, 1988

To Whom It May Concern:

Rachel Kendal was a nanny for our family for four years, from the time our two boys were 2 ½ and 5 until they were 6 and 9. She is the single most extraordinary nanny / surrogate mother that I have ever known. I was completely happy with every aspect of her work with us. She anticipated our every need and satisfied all of them. My boys adore here and never in four years complained about her. She was firm, loving, respectful of them, and always sensitive to their feelings. Moreover, they think she's great fun!

We trust Rachel implicitly and with good reason – she is one of the most moral people we know, and is honest, reliable, and completely straight forward, and we all love her. She has the clearest, most accurate sense of what we needed and just pitched in and delivered.

I can't recommend Rachel highly enough. If you are lucky enough to have her work for you, your will not know how you managed without her.

Feel free to call me or my husband anytime.

Mom in D.C.

ADVENTURES OF A NANNY

CHAPTER 5

I moved to a small, well-furnished apartment in the basement of a three-story townhouse in Vienna, VA. Mom and Dad were business people who apparently made a lot of money. The home and furnishings were new. Dad drove a BMW convertible, Mom had a Jaguar, and they bought a new Jeep Grand Cherokee for me to use. This was Mom's first marriage, but Dad had been married before. They were both thirty-eight years old. Dad's first wife had custody of their dog, and she called him once a month about visitation rights with Pookie, the poodle. Of course, this made Mom furious. She complained to me and asked me what she should do. I said, "Say to him: The next time you mention your ex-wife and Pookie, I'm going to rip the top off your BMW and stick it up the tailpipe of the Jeep. I'll put your wallet in the garbage grinder. I'll turn your piano over and stomp on the keys. Do I make myself clear?" She laughed and said, "It would be out of character for me to say that." I said, "That's my point. He'll think you've got postpartum problems and will be afraid to upset you." She said, "I'll do it." A week later she winked at me as we passed in the hall and said, "I did it." I never heard anymore about Pookie during the two years that I lived there taking care of Gary.

He was a perfect baby and I adored him. He never cried, had two naps daily, and smiled most of the time. If a nap lasted more than two hours, I wakened him by rubbing his back and talking to him. He would look at me with half-closed eyes as if to say, "There's that woman again. I wonder what she wants now." I wanted more play time with him, but he was too sleepy. However, while he slept, I had plenty of time to study for the religion class I was taking at the local college. The purpose of the class was to help the students learn about the differences and similarities in world-wide religions. I was familiar with the Protestant and Catholic faiths and wanted to study eastern religions. Our teacher assigned me to visit a mosque and to report to the class what I'd observed.

As I drove east on Route 7 the next day the traffic stopped when a police car with flashing lights parked in the middle of a four-lane crosswalk. About seventy-five men, women, and children walked across the road to attend services at a mosque. I watched them as they hurried toward the minaret that was calling them to prayer. They were dressed in dark clothing and the women wore black head scarves. I decided I would visit the mosque the following Friday, which was their special day of prayer.

I thought I would go incognito, wearing a black raincoat and a black head scarf. Considering it was raining heavily, I thought I would go unnoticed with my black umbrella pulled low over my head. I went inside the front door where I saw about a hundred pairs of shoes lined up in the vestibule. Several small children stared at me as I placed the umbrella on a shelf, took off my shoes and placed them in a corner. I heard voices coming from down the hall and walked to the room and entered where I saw about twenty women sitting on the floor. They stopped talking and stared at me. I went to the back of the room, sat on the floor with my back against the wall and stared back at them. They slowly turned around and whispered to each other as they glanced at me. I definitely was not incognito. I was embarrassed and I realized why I stood out in the crowd: I was the only woman in the room with bangs. The other women's hair was completely covered with a black scarf. I walked out of the room, put my shoes on, got into my car, and laughed at myself. When I reported the escapade to my class, they also laughed at me. However, I learned about the peaceful Muslim doctrine, and spent several hours in personal conversation with a Muslim woman who attended our class. We discussed similarities in the Muslim and Christian faiths, and the Koran, the sacred book of Islam, believed to be the word of God as dictated to Muhammad and written down in Arabic.

For Halloween, I dressed Gary in a bunny costume and took him to visit Josh and Zack. The boys were fascinated with him. They had never played with a baby, and they carried him around the house showing him all of their toys. Gary loved the attention. The new nanny had been working with other children in DC for twelve years, and was competent in handling the two boys and their schedules. I was happy to see that she had become acclimated to the household. We went out to the Zebra Restaurant for pizza and the boys played table-top games while I chatted with their nanny. It was a pleasant visit and I promised to keep in touch.

A few days later I was sitting in a nearby park with Gary beside me in his stroller when a woman with a baby walked up and said, "Hi, remember me?" I hadn't seen her in three years, but I remembered Lois. She was one of the nannies I knew from ADCAN. She had moved to Leesburg for a nanny position and stopped attending our meetings because it necessitated a long drive through rush-hour traffic at 6 p.m. As we conversed I was surprised to learn that she had married a cousin of her former employer, and was holding her own two-year-old baby girl, Tina. She was obviously six-months pregnant, and happy about her life. We were eager to renew our friendship, and made plans to take the children to the National Zoo in DC the following week. Tina was very bright and talked incessantly to Gary who didn't say much, but seemed to understand what Tina said to him.

Lois had a baby girl in January and named her Sharon. Gary and I visited them weekly because the weather was too cold to take baby Sharon to the park. Everything seemed to be running smoothly when the grandparents from Utah came to visit and play with Gary. They brought several toys that were not age-appropriate for him. He was just beginning to walk and couldn't use the tricycle. The puzzles and books were for older children. Of course, he would like those toys in about six months, so I put them in the storage room in the basement. The grandparents wanted Gary to call them "Fifi" and "Papa"; but considering he couldn't even say mama and dada yet, he just stared at their lips when they tried to teach him their names. They didn't know much about babies.

Gary's parents and grandparents decided to visit relatives in Dallas, TX for Thanksgiving and insisted that I go with them to help care for Gary. Two days before Thanksgiving we flew out of Dulles Airport in a festive mood; but by the time we arrived in Dallas we were exhausted from holding Gary and having him romp on us. We agreed that he would have his own seat on the flight back home. That night Gary slept in his parents' room—or rather, he was supposed to sleep. When I went into the kitchen the next morning at 7 a.m. Dad was sitting at the table drinking coffee and Gary was sitting in a high chair eating toast. Dad said, "If I'd known babies stayed up all night, I wouldn't be a father; his mom and I had to take turns sleeping last night." "Oh, he had a bad night?" "No, *we* had a bad night. He had a good night." I said, "Go back to bed, I'll take care of him." Of course, Gary was tired and sleepy now, so I gave him a bottle, held him while I watched the morning news, and he fell asleep. During the three hours that he slept, I rolled his crib into my room so I could take care of him at night. His aunt had provided a crib, playpen, high chair and car seat for him. The next day he adjusted to his new surroundings and slept through the night thereafter.

The next evening about sixty guests arrived at the house for a barbecue. They wore cowboy hats and boots and danced half the night. Gary and I watched the

96

frolicking on the patio from our upstairs bedroom window until he fell asleep at 11 p.m. The next day Dad said to me, "I want you to teach my son to do the Texas Two-Step. I said, "Okay, as soon as he can walk; and then I'll teach him to eat pinto beans and drink black coffee." That was a prerequisite to make certain that he grew up to be a big man in Texas. We laughed.

The next evening everyone went out to the theater except Gary and me. After Gary fell asleep, I began to read one of Margaret Truman's Capital Crime Mysteries, *Murder at National Cathedral*. About an hour later I heard a strange noise coming from the hallway. I opened the door, looked down the fifty-foot hallway, didn't see anything out of order, closed and locked my door and went back to reading. Ten minutes later, I heard the noise again. I opened my door and walked down the hall past four bedroom doors, until I heard the noise coming from a partly opened bathroom door. I knocked on the door, and when nobody answered, I quickly pushed the door open and switched on the light. I saw a sleeping, snoring beagle on a large pillow. I didn't disturb him. I went back to my room, locked my door and slept until Gary got up at 7 a.m.

On Thanksgiving day everyone helped prepare dinner and the kitchen camaraderie flowed with the champagne they were drinking. The next-door neighbors joined us at 7 p.m. and we had a superb feast. During the next few days we attended a polo game, visited a cattle ranch, shopped in a department store, ate at a Tex-Mex restaurant and played Scrabble and pool in the recreation room. On the flight home, Gary had a three-hour nap in his car seat which was buckled onto the plane seat.

As we made plans for Christmas, I was in a quandary as to what to give Mom, Dad and Gary. Finally, I decided to take pictures of Gary with my 35mm camera. He had many outfits of clothing, so I picked ten of the most attractive, dressed him and got some great shots. I wrote a comment on each picture, put them in a small album and gave it to Mom and Dad so they could carry it around to show off their handsome son.

They went to Vail, CO to ski for five days while I kept Gary, and spent time with Lois and her children. The weather was too cold for outdoor activities so we played in Lois' basement playroom, which contained toys and exercise equipment for all of us. Thankfully, the weather got warmer and we started going to the park in early March, meeting with other children and their moms or nannies.

I went to see my mother for the Easter weekend and we had fun visiting relatives. Mother was eighty-two years old and beginning to decrease her activities. She no longer drove her car and we sold it to a neighbor. We hired a housecleaning service and a home health aid to help her on a weekly basis and she was content with those arrangements. Her next door neighbors could see into her kitchen window, and checked on her every morning as she had breakfast. They were retired and spent time gardening and shopping with my mother.

On August 8 we celebrated Gary's first birthday in the park with his neighborhood playmates. On exceptionally hot days I put two inches of water in a kiddie pool and turned on a sprinkler in the backyard for the children to play with.

In September, I attended a two-day conference at Mount Saint Mary's College in Emmitsburg, MD, where I gave a lecture on dream interpretation and sold thirty of my books.

During the next six months Gary grew into a big, husky boy who could crawl up into the Jeep and get into his car seat by himself. He sang and danced the Texas Two-Step with me, and we enjoyed the pinto beans and black coffee together. However, our fun time was coming to an end because his parents bought a home near Dallas and they expected to move there as soon as the decorators finished painting. They asked me to go with them, but I declined because I wanted to stay in the DC/VA area where I had family and friends. I helped them pack and drove them to Dulles Airport thinking I would never see Gary again. The only hard part about being a nanny is that

I have to leave the children I love as my own. I tell myself it's better to have loved them and lost them, than not to have known them at all. Then I get another nanny assignment, and more children to love as soon as possible so I don't have time to grieve over my loss.

November 26, 1989

Re: Rachel Kendal

To Whom It May Concern:

Rachel Kendal was attentive and caring for my child and he adored her from the very first day of her employment with us. She was an excellent teacher for Gary. He is well ahead developmentally for his age.

Rachel is an outstanding nanny who is excellent with children. I would highly recommend her as a "trusted guardian" for any child.

She also runs an efficient and organized household. She is prompt, clean, courteous, flexible, caring, decisive, and energetic.

She was with our family for almost two years and we have never had a complaint about her.

Mom in Vienna, VA

ADVENTURES OF A NANNY

CHAPTER 6

My nanny agency called with an offer from a dad who said he needed a nanny with a college degree to care for his two little girls because his ex-wife disapproved of his present nanny, and was threatening to take them away from him. I told her to have him call me. He lived near Richmond, VA about a two-hour drive down I-95, and I didn't want to waste my time going for an interview until I knew more about what the job entailed.

When he called we talked for a few minutes about my credentials, and he asked if I was a Christian. I said "yes," and he asked me to recite John 3:16. I replied, "For God so loved the world ... should I go on?" He said, "Do you know the Twenty-third Psalm?" I responded, "The Lord is my shepherd; I shall not want..." He said he followed Jerry Falwell's way of Christianity. I said I studied world-wide religions and didn't follow anybody; but respected everybody. He said, "Okay." I could have told him that it was illegal for him to question me about my religion on an interview; but he was a lawyer and already knew that.

I met with his sister, Kay, who lived nearby, for a preliminary interview, and her opinion of the type of nanny needed. Then, I made an appointment to meet Dad for lunch at a shopping mall near his house. He didn't want his present nanny to know he was going to replace her until he found another one. I was overwhelmed with pity when I saw him. He was tall and extremely underweight, with a full beard and mustache covering most of his face. His glasses were so thick that I found it difficult to make eye contact with him. I knew immediately that he and his girls needed me. We made a quick visit to his home while nobody was there and I agreed to be the girls' nanny in a couple of weeks. When the nanny was told she was being replaced, she got angry and left immediately. Dad's sister, Kay, stayed with the girls until I arrived two weeks later.

The girls, three-year-old Sissy and eight-year-old Madison, were beautiful and well-mannered. They were healthy, happy, and obviously well-cared for. The home was large, beautiful, and well-kept. However, I didn't have separate living quarters. I shared a bathroom with Sissy. Madison's suite was next to my bedroom, and Dad had a suite at the other end of the house. The arrangement was okay with me because I wanted to be near Sissy in case she woke up at night. This job was more that of a substitute mommy, rather than a nanny. Their mommy lived a half hour away. She took them out for dinner on Wednesdays, and kept them every other weekend. I had weekends free. Dad came home at four o'clock every day and played with the girls while I made dinner. I cooked what they liked to eat, and Dad started to gain weight. Within three months he gained twenty pounds, shaved off his beard and got new glasses. He looked healthy and more relaxed than when I first met him.

We settled into the household routine: I drove the girls to school in the family van, shopped for groceries, tidied the house, did one load of laundry daily, and relaxed for a couple of hours watching television or reading in the afternoon, before picking up the girls. Mom called the girls every day after school. She was too ill sometimes to take them out, and I sympathized with her during the two years I stayed there.

When school was out in the summertime the maid came twice weekly to clean, do laundry and shop for food so I would have lots of free time to entertain the girls. They needed new clothes often because they were growing so fast, so we shopped for hours, had lunch and watched television, played Scrabble, card games, and read a book every day. They had girlfriends who visited and played with dolls and other toys. Madison went away to camp with the Girl Scouts for a week and Sissy and I read a lot. She was reading very well for a four-year-old and we got several books from the library each week. I was surprised at her singing ability. Her mother had taught her to sing about twenty hymns. She had a sweet voice and knew the lyrics verbatim. I remembered the music from my childhood and sang along with her. Of course we sang for our own enjoyment; we didn't want an audience.

Dad took the girls and me for a weekend trip in the Blue Ridge Mountains. We spent one night in a log cabin sleeping on bunk beds, and the girls complained because there was no air conditioning. The following two nights were great in a lodge with two comfortable rooms and delicious food. We hiked in the woods and saw several wild animals: a bear, deer, a rabbit, birds, and a turkey buzzard. The trip was fun for all of us.

Dad's family owned a condominium at Virginia Beach, a two-hour drive from home. I went there occasionally to relax on weekends with a neighbor, Christine, who was a nurse at a nearby hospital. We became close friends and she went with me to Detroit twice to visit my mother during the first six months that I was with Sissy and Madison. Dad took the girls to New York, and Mom took them to Disneyland while I was on a trip to Detroit. During the summer we spent lots of time at their condominium at Smith Mountain Lake near Lynchburg, VA, where the extended family gathered to enjoy water sports. Dad's mother rented the large, five bedroom condo next door for the summer so she could be with her numerous grandchildren, ages three to twenty, including three male college students who ate a lot. There were usually at least fifteen people at mealtime, which kept a cook and a maid busy taking care of them. I helped with the cooking and we all ate well. I made two large pans of brownies every morning which were gobbled up before noon.

One day I was riding in the speedboat driven by Dad, pulling Sissy on skis. Suddenly, Sissy lost her grip and did a backward somersault in the water. I yelled, "Good trick, Sissy!" She scowled, "That was no trick," and grabbed the rope for another try. She was determined to be a champion, because Madison, who was five years older, excelled in water skiing and gymnastics. Her older cousins were experienced skiers who competed in the activities at the lake community. My favorite pastime was lying on the pontoon reading, as the boat floated aimlessly in the lake.

The three male college students (who ate most of the brownies) were bungee jumpers who jumped from a nearby bridge. I watched them once, and got upset because it was so dangerous. However, they thought it was great fun so I kept my comments to myself.

We were at the lake for six weeks, and Dad went to Lynchburg with one of his nephews once a week to visit Jerry Falwell's Liberty University. The nephew was enrolled there for the fall term. They were the only two in the whole clan who were interested in Liberty University, the Religious Right, and the Moral Majority. We seldom talked about spiritual matters, and they didn't know about my "dreams" book. However, Mom (Sissy's and Madison's mom) had read my book and we discussed her dreams which were sometimes frightening. She was an unemployed nurse who previously worked with psychotic patients; but could no longer handle the stress involved. She took the girls to her church on the weekends that they were with her, and Dad took them to his church on alternate weekends. The girls never complained about that arrangement. They knew several children in both churches and enjoyed the church activities. Every Sunday Sissy sang one of her special hymns in church.

We celebrated Dad's fortieth birthday the last week in August, then prepared to go back home to shop for school clothes and supplies before school started in September. Christine was at our house and greeted us with a burger cookout when I drove the van, pulling the speed boat, into the driveway. I had driven the last two hours of our trip home because Dad was sleepy. He and the girls lay down in the back of the van and slept. I appreciated the ready-to-eat meal because I didn't feel like cooking. Christine was my only close friend during the two years I lived with Sissy and Madison and we had fun together. Dad went back to his office, and the girls and I slipped into the school-day routine.

Our lifestyle moved along effortlessly for the next three months until the Thanksgiving celebration began. The clan met at our house for a big dinner on Thanksgiving. I planned the menu, baked pies and brownies, and cooked cranberries and vegetables. Grandmother and her maid roasted the turkey. Everything was delicious. Sixteen of us had a great time eating, telling stories, and catching up on school activities. Dad's favorite nephew was doing well at Liberty University, Madison had won first place in her sixth-grade spelling bee, and all the other cousins were happy with their classes. After dinner everyone helped clean up, then we settled down with Scrabble, Monopoly, and watching football on television.

The next day, we started making plans for the Christmas vacation. Grandmother and Dad decided to take the girls to Florida. Friends of Grandmother had invited them to spend the holidays at their beach house in Naples.

The girls were eager for sunshine and water sports. I made plans to go to Detroit. I was hoping the weather would be tolerable. I hadn't forgotten how to shovel snow, but it was not my favorite pastime.

When I arrived at my mother's house everything seemed to be in order, and she was satisfied with the help she had been getting from the maid and the neighbors. However, she had a weakness in her right hand and couldn't manipulate her can opener. I bought an electric can opener and the problem was solved. I was concerned with her lack of energy and slow gait when she moved about the house. I felt that she needed someone to live with her for companionship, but she refused to let anyone intrude in her life. I didn't press the issue, although I was worried about her well-being. She didn't want to go out, but enjoyed having people visit her. We entertained friends and relatives several times while I was there.

I contacted an A.R.E. study group nearby and we met to catch up on the latest news from Headquarters. I gave each of them a copy of my "dreams" book and they were excited about studying their dreams. I gave them an introductory lesson and told them about a few of my dreams that were in my book. Several years before I started an intense study of my dreams I had this dream:

> I'm lying in bed, sleeping on my back. I know there is a spider on the ceiling above my face. It starts to descend, hanging onto one strand of its web. It gets within three feet of my face.

I suddenly awoke, jumped out of bed, ran across the room, and switched on the ceiling light. I was terrified and my heart was pounding. I sat down in a chair, breathing hard. I glanced across the room at my bed, and indeed, there was a spider suspended from the ceiling, hovering over my pillow. My first thought was: "Somebody's watching over me; but I wish He would have told me so without scaring me half to death." I'd been studying the Edgar Cayce Readings for several years and thought extra sensory perception (ESP) was interesting, but I didn't want to be personally involved with it because it was too weird for my everyday life. I was content to let ESP happen to someone else. However, in 1979 while studying with a group of A.R.E. members in Wilmington, NC, our combined dreams became so forceful that we couldn't ignore the messages we received. We used *Dreams Your Magic Mirror* by Elsie Sechrist as a guide to interpreting the symbolism contained in our dreams. We were astonished at the revelations that were giving us a better understanding of universal laws, God's love for us, and the right path to follow while we are on earth. We studied every Friday evening for eighteen months. I had several steno pads full of notes, and we realized that there were enough dreams and interpretations to fill a book. Hence, *Following My Dreams with the Edgar Cayce Readings* by Rachel Kendal.

> "We are so captivated by and entangled in our subjective consciousness that we have forgotten the age-old fact that God speaks chiefly through visions and dreams." *Carl Gustav Jung (1875-1961)*

I believe that.

I arrived back home the day before the family returned and got everything ready to start our daily routine: grocery shopping, checking mail, and calling neighbors. The girls were tanned, and talkative about their vacation; but Dad said he was anxious to get back to the office. He had dated his secretary a few times and wanted to see her. His divorce wasn't final and he was afraid Mom might make problems for him. She was holding out for a bigger financial settlement and he was protesting. Such is life.

I had my own concerns. I felt that my mother needed someone to live with her but she disagreed with me. I called her every other day and tried to cheer her up; but I could sense that she was withdrawing from the world outside of her house and was hinting that she wanted me to live with her. I talked with her next door neighbor weekly, to get her opinion on Mother's welfare and she also thought Mother needed a companion. I was in a quandary. I didn't want to move back to Detroit but I couldn't ignore my mother's situation. I started calling her every evening and listened to her report on what she had done that day. Twice a week her neighbor took her out to lunch and to shop for a couple of hours. Most of her friends had died, and she said she wasn't going to any more funerals. She had always had a fiery temper and I didn't want to upset her by making suggestions on what she should be doing to have a more interesting life. She watched several hours of television daily and took a two-hour nap every afternoon. Since she wasn't in imminent danger, I decided to stay calm, hoping that she would consent to having a companion who could take her out daily.

In the meantime, I visited her on three weekends before the girls' spring break in March. Dad and Grandmother took the girls to Williamsburg, VA and stayed three nights in a colonial house so they could absorb the early American history. Then the clan met at Grandmother's house for three nights. I stayed with my mother for five days. As I observed her behavior and physical movements, I realized she needed me to live with her.

The following week I told Dad about my dilemma. He was very upset because he knew it would be hard for him to find someone to take over my responsibilities. I knew that it would take two women to do what I'd been doing for the past two years. We discussed possibilities, but didn't come up with anything conclusive. Dad contacted the agency that placed me and they said they would try to find someone to replace me. I assured him I would stay until we could make a smooth transition.

The girls had matured in the two years that I had cared for them, and were quite sufficient in caring for themselves. They didn't need a nanny per se, rather, a young woman with an elementary teacher's degree would suffice to be their companion. Where would we find her? Liberty University! Dad liked the idea and went to Lynchburg the next week to ask a university counselor to help him find the right young lady.

Everything worked out perfectly. Dad hired a twenty-two year old woman who agreed to report for duty in five weeks. She came to visit with us several times during the five-week period and I liked the relationship she developed with the girls. She drove them to church in the van when Dad was out of town, prepared light lunches, played board games, and gave them her undivided attention. I could see she had been trained well in dealing with young children.

Now we needed to find a housekeeper. The first woman interviewed by Dad was the right one. She would be leaving her present housekeeping job at the same time that we needed her. Her job was to be on duty from noon until eight o'clock Monday through Friday and be in charge of all household tasks, including serving dinner at six o'clock. She would not live with the family since she was married and had her own household. She visited with me several times and I explained to her how to run the house.

Mavis, the girls' companion, went to Dallas with us for five days in June to attend the wedding of Dad's niece. We stayed at a large hotel where the reception was held. Madison was the flower girl, with a fever; but managed to get through the ceremony before I took her to the hotel doctor. She got antibiotics and I stayed in our room with her until Mavis came, so I could go downstairs to the reception. I saw the college guys, who greeted me with bear hugs, and said in unison, "Did you bring any brownies?" I laughed. We all had fond memories of our vacation at Smith Mountain Lake. Madison recovered overnight and we partied for two more days before we flew home.

I stayed with the girls three days after Mavis and Ella, the housekeeper, reported for duty. They seemed to understand how to handle the household, and I felt comfortable about leaving. I went to northern Virginia and stayed with Lois while I visited with friends for two weeks, because I didn't know if I'd ever be back to that area again.

2/23/92

Re: Rachel Kendal

Rachel has cared for my daughters for two years and I've found her to be a kind and gentle nanny/teacher who respects and loves children. The girls have been happy with her. I'm a divorced lawyer and my job often requires me to be away overnight. I feel comfortable leaving my children with her.

She has extraordinary managerial skills and makes efficient us of her time. She was able to run the daily affairs of my home, cook delicious meals, and still take care of the children's needs. I believe she can adapt to any household situation and do an outstanding job.

Dad in Virginia

2/22/92

Dear Rachel,

Although you've only been here two years, you have left a significant mark in all of our lives. You are a consummate nanny, house manager, and homemaker with a commitment to excellence. You have gone beyond the call of duty and been a friend to my children and me. God knows how much I needed you in April of 1990, and His provision of you to this family was indeed an answer to prayer. It's now apparent that God is calling you elsewhere, so I release you back to Him – may He direct you with the wind at your back and the sun (or Son, I should say) at your face. Thank you for your labor, your perseverance and your love.

Dad in Virginia

ADVENTURES OF A NANNY

CHAPTER 7

I arrived at my mother's house the last week in June. I knew she was feeling good because her garden was in full bloom, and the lettuce bed was full of ready-to-eat lettuce, which I ate every day. I helped her with garden chores, took her shopping, entertained relatives and friends, and we had a good relationship for about three months, until the weather got too cold to work outdoors. After we prepared the garden for winter, she got restless and cranky. I tried to appease her; but she criticized me almost daily. When a neighbor told me that her sister was looking for a part-time nanny, I applied for the job so I could give my mother space to herself, and still keep an eye on her.

I went for an interview at an estate about a one-hour drive north of Detroit in Troy, Michigan. I met Mom, Dad, and three-year-old Rebecca. Mom was a dentist, Dad was a lawyer, and Rebecca was a quiet little girl with dark eyes and black curls who ignored me during the two-hour interview, while she sat on the floor talking to her dolls. They needed me to stay with Rebecca from 9:30 a.m. Monday until 7:30 p.m. Wednesday every week. Rebecca's parents and grandparents would take care of her when I wasn't with her.

The following week I moved into a room and bath adjoining Rebecca's suite. Her suite consisted of a bedroom, bathroom, playroom, and kitchenette. We were on the third level of a large house on a hillside, overlooking several acres of cornfields which belonged to our neighbor whose house was about a mile from us. There were no children in our area for Rebecca to socialize with, so I took her to a playgroup in the nearest town which was a half-hour drive from home. Needless to say, I felt isolated and was glad to leave on Wednesday evenings to get back to my friends and the shopping mall.

As I observed Rebecca with the playgroup it was evident that she didn't know how to interact with other children. Obviously, her former babysitters hadn't given her the attention she needed. We went to the playgroup each morning for two hours, came home for lunch, played outdoors for an hour, and read a book of her choice. She memorized the books and told me the stories. Within a month she became very talkative and we invited little girls from the playgroup to come home with us for lunch. Their moms were delighted with Rebecca's outdoor playground equipment, toys, and space to run in, and I was happy to see Rebecca having a good time with her friends.

Rebecca's dog, Marmaduke, was named after the cartoon character, because he looked like him: a Great Dane, 30 inches tall, weight 100 pounds, and he was just a playful puppy. He had been to obedience classes, but he didn't learn much. He couldn't run fast enough to catch the squirrels that teased him when we played outdoors because his long, skinny legs went in different directions. When the beeper sounded at the main gate—indicating a car was approaching the house—he ran to great the car, barking until it stopped. He watched Rebecca and her friends and they adored him. He was very much like the cartoon character, making us laugh every day.

We woke up on the morning of November first, and were disappointed to see a foot of snow covering our world. I called the snow removal service and they said they would dig us out that afternoon. Mom and Dad planned to leave as soon as the driveway was cleared. Mom went upstairs to her home office. Rebecca and I watched Sesame Street, painted elbow macaroni, and made necklaces. Dad spent the morning in the exercise room to improve his muscles. He was tall and thin and often wore thermal underwear under his shirt to make him appear more muscular. He also wore boots and a fedora a la Indiana Jones, and tried to impress people with his imaginary superiority. During the two years that I cared for Rebecca, I avoided him as much as possible. I pitied Mom for being subservient to him. She was beautiful, intelligent, and earned more money than he did, so why did she tolerate his inappropriate behavior?

After lunch we heard the snow plow coming up the driveway, and ran to the front window to watch the noisy activity. Duke barked loudly in his confusion; he wanted to go outside and chase it. It was too cold to play outside, so Rebecca and I watched biblical videos of "Jewish heroes" because she would soon be attending religion classes at a nearby synagogue. The snow melted a few days later and I went to town to shop and register for yoga classes on Monday evenings. When I came out of my first class it was snowing hard. After a half-hour drive, I turned off the road into our driveway and stopped abruptly when I saw a deer standing in front of the car. The sudden stop made the car slide on the uphill driveway into a shallow ditch which was full of snow and ice. Evidently, the Mercury station wagon wasn't going anywhere that night. I walked the 300 yards uphill, slipping repeatedly. I was still in a yoga mood and kept smiling. The poor deer was still standing in the driveway afraid to move. The next morning when I answered the telephone at 6:30 a.m., the man with the snow plow informed me that he had pulled the Mercury out of the ditch and there was no damage on it. That started my day with a smile. On the next Monday evening the weather was clear and I was relaxing on my yoga mat at the YMCA when I heard a loud, unidentifiable noise coming from the hallway. The teacher left the room to check the source of the disturbance.

Coming back into our room, she said, "They're clogging next door." However, I did finish the eight yoga classes with a reasonably peaceful attitude.

Rebecca's fourth birthday was on Thanksgiving day and her family and friends celebrated at home. Grandmother was a great cook, and Dad, who fancied himself a cook, offered to help her prepare dinner. I spent that weekend with my mother and took her and the next-door neighbors out for a big Thanksgiving dinner. Mother seemed to have a better attitude toward me, now that I didn't see her every day. Of course I could sense when she was getting grouchy, so I left the house to shop, go to a movie or meet a friend for coffee. Every Friday evening I went to the A.R.E. study group meeting. We became a close-knit group for about three years. It was comforting to share my beliefs with like-minded people who studied the Edgar Cayce Readings with me. We assisted others in forming three more study groups and had a great time together.

Rebecca didn't need me for two weeks at Christmas time when she went to Vail, CO to ski with her parents, so my friend, Sally, and I went to Sarasota, FL to soak up some sunshine. It was wonderful to feel the warmth of the sun as we lay on the beach. We had Christmas dinner at a nice restaurant in Siesta Key. We ate breakfast at our hotel every morning, then went exploring up the coast at

Tampa, Clearwater, Port Richey, and Crystal River. The funniest sight we saw was a pink flamingo pulling Santa's sled. We came back home looking tanned and healthy.

I reported for work on Monday morning and Rebecca and I discussed our vacation activities. She enjoyed the snow in Vail, I enjoyed the sunshine in Sarasota. We read books, made cookies with play dough, then decided to make real cookies. I put the ingredients on the counter and set the oven temperature. I opened the oven door and slammed it shut immediately! Something inside the oven made me recoil in disgust. It looked like a furry gray animal in a baking pan. I was upset, but didn't mention it to Rebecca. Luckily there were two ovens in the kitchen. I cautiously opened the door of the second and exhaled when I found it empty. We made oatmeal cookies and went outside with Duke while they cooled on the counter. When we came in Duke grabbed a cookie before I could put them in the cookie jar. Duke had stayed with Rebecca's grandparents during our vacation and he missed us. He stayed within touching distance of Rebecca all day.

When Dad came home I told him there was something awful in the oven. As we stood ten feet away, he opened the oven and stepped back, emitted a few expletives, picked up the baking pan, and took it outside to the trash can. I said, "What was that?" He replied, "A baked chicken carcass from two weeks ago." I was glad he could identify it.

Dad really thought he could cook, even though we wouldn't eat his culinary offerings. The mess he made in the kitchen ruined our appetites. One morning I went into the kitchen when he was preparing breakfast and observed the over-heated oven, the open fridge door, the splattered cabinets from the mixer going at full speed, and Duke standing on his hind legs licking the counter. I said, "I'm glad the maid will be here soon. The crickets under the stove are having a field day. They took up residence there last week. I stuck the vacuum cleaner hose under there but couldn't reach them. I got down on all fours and beamed a flashlight at them. They were standing in a row, with their legs locked to each other, staring back at me." Dad gave me a withering look as he continued stirring the contents of a boiling pot with a wooden spoon. He dipped a spoonful, pointed it at my face and said, "Taste this." I replied, "Oh no, it's too hot." He stuck it in his mouth and licked the spoon. I said, "You must have an asbestos tongue." He started running around the kitchen yelling. I said "What's the matter? Did you burn your tongue?" He said, "No, I got a splinter in my tongue." He ran to the bathroom and poured peroxide on his tongue. I recommended a doctor and he jumped into his car and headed for the clinic in town. When he returned two hours later, he took a sedative and went to bed. The next morning he didn't say anything before he left for work. Thereafter, we didn't mention the incident.

Dad called from his office and asked me to take Rebecca ice skating on the frozen pond in back of the house. The outside temperature was 35° but the sun was shining brightly and I doubted that the ice was safe for skating. Rebecca and I bundled up in our coats and boots and went outside to test the ice. We could see cracks in the ice, indicating that it was melting and unsafe for us to skate on. I called Dad and told him we couldn't skate, but we were going to play in the snow. He became angry and told me to take her skating with a rope tied under her arms so I could pull her out if she fell in. I told him it was possible that both of us would fall in since we would be holding hands while skating. Rebecca was just learning to skate and needed my hand to support her. I said I wouldn't expose either of us to a dangerous situation. He slammed the telephone down. I figured he needed a counselor, and that I should be on guard against his bizarre behavior. Most of the parents I had worked with were highly effective on their jobs; but sometimes at home, they were downright ignorant of children's needs.

Mom informed me that she and Dad were going to Mexico City for a week, and that her parents would check with me everyday while they were gone. Dad brought a loaded shotgun to my room and told me I would be safe with it to protect me. I put it in the back of my closet without any comment. I was afraid of guns; but thanks to watching my nephews cleaning and loading their shotguns during hunting season, and advising me on target practice with a Remington 1100, I knew I could use a shotgun if necessary. However, I depended on my friend, Duke, to fend off intruders. Most people were afraid to go near him because he liked to put his paws on their shoulders and lick their faces. He was well-behaved with the family; but loved to greet strangers by jumping on them with his legs flopping around in opposite directions.

I was delighted when my friend, Sally, offered to stay with me while Mom and Dad were in Mexico City. She settled into a guest room next to my room and we had fun. We shopped while Rebecca was in the playgroup, had lunch with her at home or in a restaurant in town, and played outdoors with Duke. There was an invisible fence surrounding the house to keep Duke nearby so he wouldn't wander off and get lost. It consisted of a buried cable that emitted a low electrical current which was uncomfortable for Duke when he got within five feet of it. A receiver on his collar warned him when he was close to the fence line. However, when he was running too fast to stop at the fence line, he would go over it and keep running. When he wanted to come back to the house, he would stand at the line and bark until I turned off the current and called him to come home. When I saw him running toward the house, I ran inside so he wouldn't run over me. He tried to be obedient, but he couldn't stop quickly, and he outweighed me by five pounds. One of Rebecca's "household chores" was to watch him through binoculars from her playroom window and inform me if he was on the other side of the fence. When we sped off in the golf cart down to the main gate every afternoon to get the mail, Duke ran after us and we carried him back to the house exhausted and panting in the cart. He reminded me of three-year-old boys in preschool who were learning to control themselves. They try, but often fall short of classroom rules. Of course, that's what makes them so lovable.

Sally and I had been studying the Edgar Cayce Readings for twenty years and discussed many of the concepts contained in the *Search for God* book. We shared our dreams and helped each other with the interpretations. After Rebecca went to sleep, we prayed and meditated. The week was filled with exhilarating experiences for the entire household.

When Mom and Dad returned I noticed a copy of my "dreams" book in her carry-on bag. I asked her if she had time to read it while on vacation. She replied, "Yes, I read it all, and I have some questions for you when we can be alone for a serious discussion." I said, "Anytime you're ready." Later that week she gave the book to Grandmother, who had very disturbing dreams. I told her I would help them with interpretations. However, during the following two months they studied together and began to understand their dreams without my input. I was pleased with their progress.

One afternoon Rebecca and I had just returned from grocery shopping and were taking the bags from the garage to the kitchen when the gate alarm alerted us to a car approaching the house. We looked down the hill to see a police car driving 50 mph toward the house. I was stunned and stood by the garage waiting for an explanation. Two policemen came toward me yelling, "What are you doing here?" I said, "I'm taking groceries into the kitchen. I live here." He said, "The burglar alarm alerted the operator that there's a break-in here. You stay outside while we check the house." They drew their guns and went through the garage into the kitchen. Rebecca, Duke, and I huddled together at the corner of the garage until they came out ten minutes later. Rebecca stood behind me and peeked at them while I held Duke's collar so he wouldn't jump on them with slobbery kisses. They told me there was no one in the house; but that they had found a dead bird on the patio that had apparently flown into the picture window, setting off the burglar alarm. They didn't look happy as they drove away. Rebecca and I hurriedly put the groceries away and went upstairs to watch television in her playroom while Duke slept beside us. We didn't need any more excitement for that day.

Every three weeks Duke was bathed in a large van that parked in our driveway and gave him a beauty treatment. He liked it and cooperated with the man treating him. He came out of the van looking great with a red bow on his neck and slept all afternoon. Between treatments Dad cleaned him with dry shampoo, and vacuumed his hair. He loved it and sat motionless while being groomed.

Springtime! Rebecca and I were excited about planting flowers near the gate entrance so visitors would see them. We went to the nursery and bought a dozen each of marigolds and multi-colored zinnias. The man who cut the grass prepared the soil and we planted the flowers in one afternoon. Rebecca was a natural gardener. She enjoyed working with her hands in the soil. She talked incessantly about flowers as she scooped out the soil, put a plant in the hole, then covered the roots and firmly pressed them into place. Duke stayed nearby, watching us as we were doing this unusual task. I was hoping he wouldn't dig them up. He had two favorite spots for digging. One of them was a sandy area near Rebecca's swing, the other was a rock pile near the invisible fence line where a garter snake sunbathed on a rock until it was aware of Duke nearby, then it disappeared between the rocks. This frustrated Duke, and he tried to move the rocks around with his forepaws. I doubted that he could catch it. Once he caught a frog and played with it as if it were a ball. I distracted him with a doggie treat, grabbed it and put it over the fence line. Duke gave me a puzzled look as if to say, "Why did you take away my toy?" When he saw deer at the salt lick beyond the fence line he barked, but didn't run after them. He had learned that the warning from his collar receptor meant pain would follow if he didn't stop. He was well trained after several months of obedience school, and followed our commands precisely. It was delightful to see Rebecca bossing him around. He was very gentle with her.

132

Rebecca started religion classes once a week at the synagogue. She was excited to be studying the Bible stories with her classmates. Her teacher told me she was the only pupil in her class that had prior knowledge of the Bible. I explained that Rebecca had a serious interest in the Bible for one so young, and that I enjoyed teaching her. She said, "My Dear, you are a mensch." That was the best compliment I had ever gotten. I felt that I had done a good job teaching Rebecca as a preschooler, and now she was ready to enter kindergarten at a prestigious school with other privileged children. Mom and I had discussed Rebecca's progress often during the two years that I cared for her and I thought she understood Rebecca's needs Rebecca would also do well with input from her teacher and grandmother. She knew that I would be leaving her in September; but that we would have fun until I left, and I would be back to visit her.

One afternoon we were playing in the yard with Rebecca's friends when we saw three hot-air balloons drifting toward us! We got excited! We stood there in amazement as they drifted overhead and the people aboard waved to us. The swooshing sound of the hot air being pumped into the balloon scared Duke and he sat beside my feet leaning on me while we watched until they were out of sight. At last, this was my chance for a balloon ride! We told Mom about the balloons and she offered to get me a ticket to ride. She knew the owners of the balloons.

Two weeks later, I met with several others at a balloon launching site about five miles from home. Four balloons were being prepared to go up. I was a little apprehensive when I saw them lying flat on the ground. They looked deflated and vulnerable. I was dubious about the safety of the balloons. However, I reminded myself that this was my only chance for a balloon ride. We were briefed about proper behavior while aboard and told to follow instructions from the pilot. I was in a balloon with five other people and my 35mm camera. As we drifted through the sunset, the view was breathtaking. I got some beautiful pictures. As we passed over a large chicken house, the chicken were frightened. We could hear them squawking as they ran for cover. A herd of deer eating corn in a large field were startled, and ran into a stand of oak trees as we passed over them. Several people waved to us. After a one-hour flight, we received directions on where to land, through a two-way radio in a van driving below us. We landed with a thud, the wicker basket on its side with all of us either sitting or lying on each other, but nobody was hurt. I decided one balloon ride was enough for me. We rode back to the launching site in the van, had a cheese and wine party, and laughed about the landing. I had satisfied my curiosity about balloons; and now, some down-to-earth problems were looming on the horizon.

Dad was making an exhibition of his bizarre behavior and anger, and I assumed he had emotional problems. One morning he told me that Mom was cheating him out of his money. Rebecca was playing near the kitchen table where we were sitting. I told Dad it was not my business, and he shouldn't say anything that would upset Rebecca. He left for work and didn't mention it again. A few days later, Rebecca and I were in her playroom, and I picked up the binoculars and looked across the yard to the fence line to check on Duke. I saw Dad walking toward Duke. Duke was sitting quietly on the grass and Dad walked up to him and kicked his left leg. I was stunned! I quickly ran downstairs and out the front door calling Duke. Duke ran to me and I took him upstairs to be with Rebecca. I came back to the kitchen and told Dad that if I saw him abuse Duke again, I'd call the Humane Society and report him. That evening I told Mom about the incident and she said she would speak to him. I was furious, but felt helpless about doing anything to solve problems in the household.

The following week while Rebecca and I were reading I heard a gunshot from outside the house. I cautiously looked out of the window and saw Dad below with his shotgun. I opened the window and said, "You shouldn't fire a gun so close to the house." He said, "I wanted to get a pheasant. Hunting season opened today." Of course, it was legal for him to shoot the birds; but illegal to fire a gun that close to a residence. I figured he was just trying to annoy me. I told Mom, and I never heard any more guns fired near the house. I knew I would be leaving soon and be rid of these problems.

Mom asked me to stay with Rebecca on Thursday morning because her patient needed minor surgery in her office. I agreed and she left at 6 a.m. I was in the kitchen when Dad came downstairs at 8 a.m. all dressed up. He was wearing high-heeled boots, a fedora, tan pants and shirt, with a red kerchief tied around his neck. I could see the outline of the thermal undershirt that made him look muscular. I did not like this show-off, and my hostility was burning my tongue. He said, "How do I look?" I said, "You look like an Indiana Jones wannabe; but you're not gonnabe."

At that moment the gate alarm sounded the arrival of a car in the driveway, and Dad went outside. A few minutes later he came in, got Rebecca, and took her out to the car. Rebecca came back in and he went away in the car. I said, "Who was that?" She said, "Daddy's girlfriend." I didn't respond, and distracted her with: "Hey, let's make pancakes!"

The following week I went into the kitchen at 6 a.m. and found Mom crying. She said, "Dad left last night. He wants a divorce." I wasn't surprised because I actually thought she was too good for him; but I just said, "Let me know if I can help you." She didn't want to talk and soon left for work. Mom's parents called me because they were upset. I told them I didn't know what was going on. They had noticed Dad's strange behavior for several months, and of course, they wanted their daughter to be safe. Dad returned four days later and nobody mentioned his absence during the two days he spent packing his clothes and exercise equipment, then departing with a loaded U-Haul truck. I smiled as he drove away. I exhaled, realizing a stressful situation was over for me. Mom didn't mention her problems to me even though I stayed in touch with her for a year after I left there. She bought a smaller house closer to her office and I helped her move. Her parents were very helpful with the transition. Thankfully, I never heard a word about Dad's escapades after the divorce. Mom remarried to an orthodontist with two children and they seemed to be a happy family. The children were in a private school. They had a good nanny and competent housekeeper. I wished them the best.

Re: Rachel Kendal

During the two years that Rachel cared for my daughter, Rebecca, she was energetic, enthusiastic, loving, and consistent with her.

I strongly recommend Rachel as a nanny and would have kept her in my employ if not for my daughter going to kindergarten. She has been an extremely dutiful, reliable, likable, and fun nanny. My daughter has benefitted from her care both emotionally and intellectually. Her background in child development and her experience as a nanny has made her an excellent caregiver.

I cannot say enough about Rachel as an employee and as a person and, again , would strongly recommend her as a caregiver.

Mom in Troy, MI
October, 1994

ADVENTURES OF A NANNY

CHAPTER 8

In October of 1993 I went to take care of two towheaded little angels. Amber was three years old and big brother, Timmy, was four. Both of them had golden curls and big blue eyes. They were healthy, happy, and delightful to be with. During the sixteen months that I was with them, their preschool teachers were amazed at their intellectual progress. Timmy finished the kindergarten requirements, and went directly from preschool to first grade. Amber was at the top of her class in kindergarten.

Their home was located in Bloomfield Hills, MI, which was only fifteen minutes from Rebecca and her mom. I kept in touch with them and took Rebecca to lunch and shopping about once a month.

This household was very different from my previous job where I was not compatible with the dad. Amber and Timmy's dad adored them and consulted with me often about their care and education. I soon learned that Mom was manipulative toward Dad, the children, and me. She owned a small business with six employees, and apparently made a large salary; but a few times she tried to cheat me on my time sheet which was posted inside a kitchen cabinet door. I worked four days per week and was paid by the hour. I had a nice room and bath on the third level of a large home on lake front property with a private beach. When I stayed overnight I was comfortable, but I did not consider my job to be my home. Mom was often late coming home from work and I marked my time sheet according to the hours I spent with the children while she talked on the phone, groomed herself in her bathroom, jogged outside, read a magazine, or whatever she did that took her attention away from the children. When the parents went out in the evening I sat in the room with the sleeping children and read until they came home. This usually extended my work day to fifteen hours in a twenty-four hour period. Of course, I expected to be paid for fifteen hours and marked my worksheet accordingly. When I noticed she had altered my account to her benefit, I told her I would leave if she did that again. She got my point; but I kept an accurate record in my room just in case I had to confront her again.

I usually took the children to preschool at 9 a.m., then went to have coffee and conversation with Denise, a former army nurse who was now a nanny for a ten-year-old boy. She didn't mince words when talking about incompetent parents, and was ready to give her opinion on any subject; but I liked her and we laughed a lot together. After coffee, I went to the library to borrow children's books, then shopped for groceries. At home I tidied the areas in the house that the children used, did their laundry, and tried to prepare nutritious meals. Mealtime was a challenge for all of us. Mom let them eat anything—or nothing—and after I was there three months she was still feeding them frozen food—and I do mean frozen. Timmy's favorite food was uncooked hot dogs covered with ice crystals, and frozen peas just out of the freezer which he ate with his fingers. Amber usually mimicked his eating habits. However, their teachers said they ate well at school and their doctor said they were healthy, so I did my best in feeding them, and also gave them one-a-day vitamins.

I volunteered to help decorate their school room for Halloween, and read a spooky story at the party. It was fun to see the wide-eyed wonder on their faces when ghosts started flying around the darkened room. Of course, they didn't know the teachers were manipulating white sheets on broomsticks.

For Thanksgiving, Mom asked me to go to the Florida Keys with the family to visit friends. She promised me a room of my own, free time, and a rented car so I could explore the islands. I agreed to go and we left two days before Thanksgiving. Our hostess was very gracious in helping us settle into a guest house in the back of a mansion which faced the ocean. The refrigerator and cabinets were well-stocked, and I made lunch for the children.

I got my first inclination of trouble when I saw Mom and Dad's luggage in my room. I soon learned that all of the guest rooms in the big house were filled and Mom and Dad would take my room. I slept on the living room couch during the week we were there.

On our first night in Key Largo, Amber woke up screaming with an earache. Mom and Dad took her to a nearby clinic where she got some antibiotics. She felt better the next day and we played on the beach. The Thanksgiving feast was delicious and I took leftovers to the guest house. When we had eaten everything and the cupboards were bare, I asked Dad for the car keys so I could go buy groceries. He said I couldn't drive the car because it was insured for only him to drive. Reluctantly, he drove me to the grocery store. Mom hadn't told him that she promised me the use of a car.

Amber was restless one night and I was up with her for several hours. Mom and Dad left the children with me while they swam, sailed, and water skied every day, then attended parties every night. Needless to say, I was tired when we returned home. The next day Mom left a check on my dresser that was two hundred dollars less than what she owed me. I told her and she immediately wrote another check for me. I felt that I couldn't trust her about anything.

Mom went on a business trip to Chicago while Dad was in Paris on business affairs. Dad came home unexpectedly and became angry because Mom had left me alone with the children for five days. They had no nearby relatives or friends that I could call in case of emergency. Of course, I had a nanny network I could depend on because I had filled in for nannies in emergencies. During my twenty-six years as a nanny, I never had a sick day!

Dad asked me to get something out of the freezer for dinner; he wanted to eat and relax at home. Amber and Timmy crawled all over him, and entertained him while I heated a large pan of lasagna and tossed a salad. After dinner he tucked them into his bed. At 6 a.m. the next morning I heard the three of them running through the house. I went downstairs and prepared breakfast. He drove the children to school and I went shopping. Later that afternoon he came and sat down in the kitchen while I was baking a cake, and poured out his anger against his wife. I really didn't want to get involved in their marital problems, but I had to stay in the kitchen and finish the cake. He sat on a kitchen stool at the counter and watched me while he talked. (He also liked to bake and we traded a few recipes.)

He said that he and Mom lived together for five years before they got married because his first wife wouldn't agree to a divorce and property settlement. He had two grown sons and didn't want another family. Mom said she didn't want children. However, he found himself at age fifty-five with two preschoolers and a forty-year-old wife who was irresponsible concerning the children. The children didn't lack for anything and were happy; but he thought she should be more motherly. The biggest problem, in my opinion, was that she was unaware of the children's needs and simply wanted them as playmates while a nanny and teachers guided and disciplined them. This was a familiar problem with all the working moms I had dealt with. They couldn't do everything they wanted to do pertaining to business and parenting, so they depended on nannies and teachers. Dads couldn't do it all either. I think most parents did their best with their children but felt lacking in some aspects of childcare. Mom came home the next day and I heard a lot of laughter between them as they played with the children. They had a lot to be thankful for.

For Christmas vacation the family planned to go to Los Angeles to visit relatives. I went to Virginia Beach, VA for a conference and a New Year's Eve party at the Association for Research and Enlightenment (A.R.E.) Headquarters. I stayed with friends who lived near Headquarters and we walked daily on the beach, which was quite cold, but refreshing. I saw A.R.E. members from around the world and gave twenty of them a copy of

Following My Dreams with the Edgar Cayce Readings to use in their dream study class. My book was popular with A.R.E. members, but I didn't make a profit on it. It was a labor of love for me. Perhaps this book I'm now writing, *Adventures of a Nanny,* is also a labor of love, but it would be nice to have a bestseller.

Everyone returned home on January 2 to begin the New Year of 1994. Amber and Timmy were eager to get back to school; Mom and Dad scheduled their business trips so at least one of them would be home all the time and I settled into the four-day-week routine. The routine was soon shattered when Mom brought home a kitten for the children. Dad was furious because she hadn't consulted him before buying it. The children mishandled the kitten on the first day, and got scratch marks on their hands and arms. I put antiseptic and Band-Aids on them. The teacher frowned disapprovingly and said they were too young to play with a kitten because they treated it like a stuffed animal and the kitten was trying to protect itself. Those were exactly my sentiments. Dad tried to explain the situation to Mom; but she insisted on keeping the kitten. The kitten managed to avoid the children most of the time by hiding in various places in the eighty-five-hundred-square-foot house. The maid complained that she found cat excrement in several rooms even though there was a kitty-litter box on each floor.

146

One day Amber threw the kitten over the balcony onto a marble floor, barely missing Dad's head. Dad rushed the kitten to the veterinarian's office and got X-rays. Luckily, it wasn't hurt; but Dad was very angry with Mom. The situation erupted when Dad discovered that kitty had been in his closet scratching his clothes. He called the vet who said he would find a good home for kitty. Dad explained to the children and everyone, but Mom, was delighted at kitty's departure after a two week residency with us.

The next day we all went bobsledding on a nearby hill. What fun! Mom was still pouting over kitty; but managed to hide her anger from the children. It was very cold, and after ninety minutes of going up and down the hill, we went home, had hot chocolate, and watched a Disney movie.

The children and I were so tired of the cold weather and heavy coats and boots that we figured out a way to escape it. We made a beach scene in an upstairs guest suite. A 4 x 8 foot gym mat covered by a beige fleece blanket, was a sandy beach on the bathroom floor. A sunlamp swiveled out of a cabinet, brightening the room. A small electric heater with a fan created a warm breeze. Water-play toys floated in the bathtub. We wore our swimsuits and put suntan lotion on our legs and arms. We were content as we lay on the "beach" eating peanut butter and crackers, and sipping juice boxes, while telling stories and conversing for an hour. Then we drained the bathtub, turned off the sunlamp and heater, leaving everything in place for the next beach visit. We had tried to replicate the beach at Key Largo, and revive the happy memories of sunny days. It was fun to use our imagination.

Mom came home from a shopping trip at the mall and informed us that she had Tim Allen's autograph. (The Home Improvement/Tool Time star on television.) She was elated. I think she had been stalking him. He lived about a mile from us. I watched his show almost every week, but I didn't want his autograph and had no interest in his private life. Mom also talked about Aretha Franklin, who lived nearby. Her chatter gave me an eerie feeling about fans stalking celebrities. However, I think she was just basically immature. Sometimes *I* stalked *her* when she was with the children. I was concerned that she would do something inadvertently to hurt them physically, like pushing them too high on a swing, or psychologically, by reading something to them that was inappropriate for their age group.

Mom made plans to take Amber and Timmy to Cedar Rapids, IA to visit relatives for their Easter vacation. Dad planned to go on a business trip to Paris. I went to my mother's to extend a helping hand with her doctor's appointments and supervise cleaning services for her house.

I took Mother and her friend to a popular restaurant for dinner on Easter Sunday, which was enjoyable for all of us. The following day the cleaning crew put the house in order with much interference from Mother. She didn't like all that "commotion" they caused. Her grouchiness disappeared when they presented her with an Easter lily to give her green thumb a jump-start for spring gardening. We discussed plans for the garden and were eager to start planting.

The next morning I took Mother to a chiropractor for a tune up on her eighty-five-year-old body. She grunted and complained as he twisted and pressed her spine, then agreed to have earwax removed. I watched from across the room as she lay on her side, a cloth over her face and hair, with only her ear visible. The doctor rolled up a piece of typing paper into a funnel, stuck it in her ear and lit the top of it with his cigarette lighter. The flames from the paper shot upward and I thought: Mother would kill him if she knew what he did. I stepped forward, intending to pull the paper out of her ear just as the doctor pulled it out and showed me two chunks of wax that had come from Mother's ear. Frankly, *I* felt like killing him. I never told Mother, and I never took her back to that witch doctor.

Later that week, Mother had a cataract removed from her left eye with no problem. She insisted on going out to lunch an hour later and never had a complaint. She seemed to have a good appetite, but was too thin and frail, so I encouraged her to eat more. I cooked whatever she wanted and kept her kitchen well-stocked. However, one day she wanted a hamburger, and I didn't have any hamburger buns. There were three inches of snow on the ground and I didn't want to drive on it. So I bundled up in heavy clothing and walked a mile to a restaurant to get carryout burgers and fries. The fresh air was invigorating and after we ate I shoveled the sidewalk. The next day was sunny, much warmer, the snow melted, and our thoughts turned to gardening. We made plans for preparing the soil and planting broccoli, lettuce, asparagus, carrots, onions, tomatoes, and peppers. We liked homegrown vegetables and grew enough to share them with our neighbors.

Mother wanted to visit the Henry Ford Museum in Dearborn, MI with several neighbors. We commandeered four wheelchairs at the entrance to the museum, and four of us pushed four elderly ladies around the museum for two hours. Mother was reluctant to get into the wheelchair, but I promised her lunch at the Dearborn Inn and she agreed. In the 1940s, she had been a waitress there and considered that era "the good old days." Most of her friends and relatives worked in factories during WWII, manufacturing tanks, airplanes, jeeps and other equipment necessary for fighting a war. Mother didn't have the required proof of citizenship to work in a "war plant." There was no record of a birth certificate in the North Carolina mountains where she was born in 1909. Her family moved to McDowell County, West Virginia in 1920, and then to Detroit in 1930.

I still had a few more vacation days before reporting to my job, so three friends and I drove to Toledo, OH to attend a weekend A.R.E. Conference. I drove the one-hour trip in a new Volvo station wagon that Dad had provided for me to drive the children in. He said it would stand up in a crash test. (We were to find out later what a well-built automobile it was.) The conference was held at a hotel where we rented the entire second floor for two nights. We had gabfests in our rooms half the night. It was fun to meet with old friends again.

Two days later I returned to Bloomfield Hills to stock the kitchen and get ready for the children's return to school. Within a few days the household settled down to normal and we were looking forward to warm weather.

One evening Dad came home and announced that we were going to Paris on June 1 for two weeks. We were ecstatic! Amber, Timmy, and I went shopping at the mall and bought new clothes. Their teachers gave me extra assignments for them to work on so they could keep up with their classes. I made arrangements for a nurse's aid to stay with my mother. Mother usually took care of herself, but I didn't want her to be alone while I was out of town. Of course, her neighbors saw her everyday, but they were also elderly and unable to help her in an emergency. Mother finally consented for the nurse's aid to stay with her and I spent a weekend with them before we left for Paris.

On June 1 at 7 p.m. Dad, Amber, Timmy, and I were sitting in a limousine in front of the house waiting for Mom to finish primping so we could be on our way to the airport. She liked to keep the limousine and driver waiting to show off for the neighbors as she came out of the house laden with beautiful clothes and jewelry. Finally, we sped down US-24 toward the Detroit Metropolitan Airport, laughing and singing preschool songs.

After a romp in the kiddie's playroom at the airport terminal, we boarded the plane. The children and I were seated behind the bulkhead, with Mom and Dad on the other side of the barrier. There was enough room on the floor in front of our seats for the children to lie down and sleep. They watched a movie with their parents, then went to sleep on the floor with their pillows and blankets. I lowered the arm rests on our three seats, curled up and fell asleep. Once during the night, I awoke when I heard a baby crying; otherwise we slept soundly.

We arrived in Paris at sunrise, piled our luggage into a taxi and went to Dad's apartment. Dad leased the one-bedroom apartment on the sixth floor of the building because he had business appointments in Paris every three weeks. From the balcony, I could see the Eiffel Tower which was about a mile away. We hurriedly freshened up and went to eat breakfast at a little sidewalk cafe. Dad knew the proprietor and spoke to him in French. Thankfully, the waitress spoke English and I ordered food that I knew the children would like.

It was exhilarating to be in Paris! Mom bought a two-seat stroller, and we took turns pushing the children as we walked for miles, observing life in the city. Being one of the premiere fashion centers and tourist destinations in the world, you can expect to find a lot of amazing things and places in Paris. One of these is Avenue des Champs-Elysees; probably the most famous avenue in the world, which is a cross world of twelve major streets, all appropriately named after French military leaders. I declined Dad's offer to let me drive his car in Paris. The cars, buses, motor bikes, bicycles, and pedestrians on the streets were too much for me to navigate.

For the first week, we made plans to go to Disneyland, take a cruise on the Seine, and visit the Louvre. While Mom and Dad took the children to

Disneyland, I took a walking tour with a group of tourists. Our guide took us on a two mile trek before lunch. We saw monuments, fountains, and statues that were overwhelming in their beauty and historical meaning.

The children slept with Mom and Dad in a king-size bed. I slept on an uncomfortable cot by the dining room table. So what—I was in Paris! We ate most of our meals at the nearby sidewalk cafe. I had no intention of cooking in that tiny kitchen with a three burner stove and a minuscule refrigerator whose door was held shut by a chair propped against it. However, it cooled milk and various snacks and we had a microwave oven, so I didn't complain. We were outside most of the daytime and weren't interested in the apartment. On our third day in Paris, Mom and I took the children to a park. Timmy and I headed for the high slide; Mom took Amber to the swing on the other side of the playground and we were out of touch for a half hour. I noticed that Amber was crying, but didn't question her. I thought Mom had settled her problem. We had lunch and went back to the apartment so the children could read and rest. Amber was crying quietly, but I wasn't aware of any problem, and I thought she was probably tired and homesick for her own room and toys. The four of us napped for an hour and Amber woke up crying with a slight fever. I gave her aspirin and she calmed down. I stayed in with her that evening while

Mom and Dad took Timmy out for dinner and a ride on the subway.

Amber slept through the night and seemed to be in a good mood as we cruised down the Seine listening to the tour guide that afternoon. At four o'clock we came back to the apartment to rest before dinner. At five o'clock all chaos broke loose as Amber was screaming and yelling that her shoulder hurt. I was alarmed and asked, "Did you fall out of bed?" She said, "No, I fell out of the stroller." Dad looked angrily at Mom and said, "Did she fall?" Mom shook her head affirmatively and said, "She didn't want to use the seat belt in the park." I immediately knew that she had been hurt during that half hour in the park when she was out of my sight with Mom. Then I became angry because I had told Mom several times to make them buckle up. She wouldn't discipline them even for their own safety.

Dad picked up Amber and said he was taking her to the hospital. He told Mom to stay home, and told me to take care of Timmy; both of them were crying. I tried to console them, but I didn't feel sympathetic toward Mom. Her lack of parental skills infuriated me. I ignored her and read to Timmy.

Two hours later, when Dad returned with Amber, he said she had a broken collarbone. He looked at Mom and said, "Get everything packed tonight; we're going home in the morning so Amber can see her own doctor." Mom and the children were crying, Dad was giving orders through clenched teeth, and I started packing. Later, I went to the cafe and brought dinner home for the children and me, and Dad and Mom went out. I'm sure it was not a pleasant dinner for them. I was devastated, but tried to be cheerful for the children.

Our flight departed at 9 a.m. with the same seating arrangements that we had before. Amber was feeling okay as she played on the floor at my feet, read her books, and napped several times. Timmy stayed with his parents during most of the flight which gave me plenty of time to evaluate the situation I was in with this family — or to be more specific — with the *mother* of this family. I was upset because we had such a short time in Paris and I didn't get to see Versailles or the Mona Lisa. I said to myself, "I will return." When we landed Dad got two taxis and took Amber to the hospital to see her doctor. Mom, Timmy and I went straight home in the other one. The doctor gave instructions for Amber's care, and we were relieved to know she would be okay.

Mom and Dad went to their offices the next morning and I was busy all day comforting the children and tending to their needs. They were so precious. I loved them and wanted to stay with them. That night I lay awake trying to figure a way out of the dilemma that confronted me. I felt that I was doing a good job in caring for the children (Dad told me so), and that Mom was undermining my efforts with her lack of common sense pertaining to childcare. She was competent in her business affairs, but a failure at home. I decided to stay with the children through the summer, working to improve the household status by teaching the children more safety rules, and to buckle up by themselves in the car and stroller. They listened intently because they understood that the rules were to keep them safe.

I gave Mom a book on basic childcare and was surprised that she wanted my input while she was reading it. I think she was trying to better understand the children's needs. She also cut her office work to three days per week and seemed to be enjoying her days with them. Dad approved of her efforts and smiled more often.

I was happy to have more time with my mother. We worked in the garden and entertained neighbors with cookouts. I also took a trip to Isle Royale in Lake Superior with my A.R.E. friends. Mike and Greta Johnson invited Sheila and me to go with them on a trip to the Upper Peninsula in Michigan. We left on a Saturday morning to avoid heavy traffic as we drove north on Interstate 25, heading for Sault Ste. Marie. After dinner that evening, we spent the night at a motel near the Soo Locks. The next day we were fascinated watching the barges, tugboats and great lakes freighters as they passed through the Locks at the twenty-foot drop between Lake Huron and Lake Superior. The Locks permit waterborne commerce between Lake Superior and the other Great Lakes.

For lunch we tried pasties, which consisted of a folded pastry case filled with meat and vegetables. We liked them. The waitress told us that the men who worked in the copper mines during the past century carried them in their lunch boxes.

We drove west on Route 28 to Route 41 at the Copper Country State Forest, then to Keweenaw to spend the night. The next morning we visited a copper mine in Delaware, MI which had flourished in the mid-1800s, but was now a ghost town. However, we didn't see any ghosts as we followed the guide through the mine with yellow hard hats bobbing on our heads. That afternoon we took a ferry from Copper Harbor to Isle Royale which is located in the northwest corner of Lake Superior. There were no cars on the Island; it was delightful to ride in a horse-drawn buggy to the Grand Hotel which was quite impressive with Victorian architecture and a long row of rocking chairs on the front porch. We stayed there two nights enjoying the spa treatments, gourmet food, and rocking on the front porch, eating chocolate fudge and gossiping. Between lectures and movies pertaining to the historical significance of the Island, we took long walking tours which increased our appetites for the next delicious meal.

The early morning ferry took us back to Copper Harbor where we stowed our luggage in the car and resigned ourselves to the long drive home. We took turns driving and napping on Routes 45, 141, and 43 as we went south in Wisconsin. Near Milwaukee, we got on Interstate 94 which took us around Lake Michigan and all the way to Detroit.

I spent the next day with Mother, then went back to take care of Amber and Timmy. We shopped for school clothes and book bags. They had outgrown most of their clothes and I enjoyed buying lots of new outfits. We played outside, swam in the neighbor's pool, and read several books every day. They were intelligent and had become self-reliant during the summer months. Dad appreciated the excellent care I had given them through their early childhood learning experiences; but Mom took credit for my work, bragging about her well-behaved children to the neighbors who didn't have nannies and were exhausted from all of their duties. I felt that the children would do well in school and that they would thrive with their Dad and another nanny looking after them. I wanted to stay with my mom because her health was failing. I talked with her doctor and he said that in addition to angina pectoris (heart trouble), diverticulitis (intestinal track inflammation), and Parkinson's disease, she needed a hip replacement. In other words, her little eighty-five year-old body was worn out. To this, I might add that she had a bad case of the grouches. I was the only one who could appease her, so I knew I would soon be leaving the children to take care of her. I told the children I would be leaving after we found another nanny for them. I explained to them that my mother needed me and assured them that I would be back to visit.

Mom and Dad interviewed six nannies and chose one to live with us under my supervision for a two-week trial period. I liked her immediately. Lisa was a thirty-year-old first grade teacher who understood the children's needs. We talked incessantly and agreed to keep in touch after I left. I felt pangs of jealousy as the children gravitated toward her the first day. I was also happy, thinking she could replace me without any harm to the children.

I was on the way to visit Mother on Thursday morning, and stopped at the red light at the intersection of US-24 and Michigan Avenue in Dearborn. In my rear view mirror I saw a pickup truck with big wheels speeding toward me. I pumped my brake pedal to warn him that cars were stopped for the red light in three lanes; but he didn't slow down. He crashed into the back of the Volvo. I heard glass shatter as I felt my seat belt press the air out of my lungs. The Volvo landed seventy-five feet away, throwing my seat into a reclining position. I managed to release the seat belt and catch my breath. A man looked at me through a broken window and said, "An ambulance will be here in a few minutes, don't move." Excruciating pain enveloped me but I remained conscious. I prayed during the ten-minute ride to the hospital and my prayers were answered. Two hours later I walked out of the hospital in good health except for a small bruise on my wrist. The Volvo had a bent frame, broken windows, smashed seat, and two flat tires. It was hauled away to the junk yard.

Three days later, Lisa and the children picked me up in a new black Jeep Cherokee and I stayed a

162

week longer with the children, assuring them that we would remain friends.

August, 1996

Re: Rachel Kendal

Rachel cared for my two children, ages 3 and 5, for eighteen months and they adore her. I found her to be very responsible and she took a very serious interest in their academic and emotional growth.

She was extremely helpful in keeping the household running efficiently. She was always courteous, flexible, decisive, and prompt. She has a great work attitude and excels in all of her duties.

I would highly recommend Rachel for trusted childcare.

Mom in Bloomfield Hills, Michigan

ADVENTURES OF A NANNY

CHAPTER 9

In her "good" days Mother and I were busy preparing the garden for winter. Bob, the man who cut the grass, did the heavy work and cleaned the leaves out of the gutters. Halloween was fun, passing out candy to kids in cute costumes. Ten of us had a potluck dinner at our house for Thanksgiving; then six of us had Christmas dinner with a neighbor. In the meantime I visited Lisa, Amber, and Timmy every two weeks for lunch. Their household was running smoothly, and the rapport between Lisa and Amber convinced me that Lisa was doing a good job.

I attended an A.R.E. weekly study group and four of us made plans to go to Virginia Beach for a New Year's Eve celebration. While we were there fifty of us signed on to take a trip to Cairo, Egypt. It took me two months to prepare for the two-week trip. I managed to take only two carry-on bags with mix-and-match clothes that I could wash and wear overnight. I called the local Board of Health and a nurse informed me that I needed to be inoculated for cholera, and that I must eat a sugar cube for protection against polio.

I was Mother's legal guardian and we had made arrangements ten years previously for her end-of-life care and funeral. I explained everything to my daughter, Linda, who agreed to care for Mother while I was on vacation. Mother's favorite nurse's aid agreed to live with her for two weeks. I would not be able to communicate with them for five days while I was sailing up the Nile River visiting ancient temples and tombs, so Linda would be in charge to make decisions in case of an emergency.

An A.R.E. friend took me to visit her sister, Beverly, who gave psychic readings. As soon as we were introduced, Beverly said, "What does Nubia mean?" I said, "I think Nubia is a country in Africa." She said, "Nubia in capital letters is floating above your head." I was puzzled, and as she gave my reading, I listened to information about my life that I had heard from several other psychics. This was proof to me that psychics had a sixth sense that they used to obtain information from the Akashic Records.

The following is an excerpt from *Edgar Cayce on the Akashic Records* by Kevin J. Todeschi:

> For more than forty years of his adult life, Edgar Cayce was able to put himself into some kind of trance state and provide individuals with accurate information, called readings, in response to virtually any question. In this state he was able to perceive a source of information which he called the Akashic Records, or "God's Book of

Remembrance." As he gave a reading, Cayce described the procedure as one in which he became a portion of the records themselves. It was while being connected to these records that all manner of information became available to him. Also called the Book of Life, this source was the compilation of every thought, word, and deed that had occurred in space and time since the dawn of creation. And it enabled Cayce to just as easily provide answers into the nature of the universe as he could give insights into an individual's mission in life or a longstanding problem.

In 1934, Cayce gave a lecture in which he emphasized the reality of the Akashic Records. He told his audience, "Don't ever think that your life isn't being written in the Book of Life! I found it! I have seen it! It is being written: YOU are the writer!" That same year one of the readings discussed the fact that these records are inscribed on some kind of "etheric energy," similar in nature to the energy of thought. Because these records are literally impressed upon energy, Cayce stated that it would eventually be possible to create a machine that could analyze this energy and subsequently "read" what the records contain (443-5)

March 2, 1995 was our departure day, and I was ready to go! From Detroit Metro Airport, I took a plane to JFK in New York, then flew non-stop to Cairo. As I emerged from the bus that took our group to a hotel, I heard someone call my name. I looked up and was surprised to see Ahmed, an Egyptologist that I knew when I lived in Virginia Beach. We had studied the Edgar Cayce Readings together, and had learned from each other. He still lived in the shadow of the Sphinx where he was born. Ahmed Fayed was the owner of Fayed International Travel in Giza, Egypt. He and John Van Auken were our tour guides and every day was exciting.

From the Cairo Airport a bus took us to the Mena House Hotel in Giza. Our group rested in the afternoon, and had dinner together at the hotel that evening.

The Mena House is an historic palace resort with a royal past, located in the shadow of the Great Pyramid. It's royal history is reflected in the luxurious interiors that are embellished with exquisite antiques, handcrafted furniture and rich textiles. A variety of international as well as Egyptian cuisine is offered at the restaurants and bars at the hotel. After dinner we were entertained by acrobats and belly dancers. That was the perfect place to begin our exploration of Cairo.

After breakfast the next morning, we toured the Giza plateau, with its three great pyramids, and a panoramic view of the queens pyramid, Isis Temple, Sphinx, and Valley Temple. That evening we meditated in the King's chamber near the top of the Great Pyramid. It was a long, arduous climb inside the 454 foot high monument but well worth the effort. I sat on the floor with my head about one foot away from the ventilator shaft on the south wall. Fifty of us were crowded into the chamber for twenty minutes, and even though the air was warm and humid, I felt privileged to be there. I went back to my room totally relaxed and had a good night's sleep.

The next day several in our group rode camels. I passed on that experience; but watched the others trying to control the beasts while they bounced around on top of them.

On the plateau we saw a group of children who smiled, and waved to us. The children speak their native tongue until they learn English in the first grade. We visited a perfume factory where I purchased several bottles; and a papyrus shop where I had my name printed in hieroglyphs on a sheet of papyrus for a souvenir.

We toured the magnificent Egyptian Museum in Cairo, and had lunch at an outdoor restaurant on the Nile. That afternoon we visited the elevated Citidel fortress which dominates the Cairo skyline, overlooking the City of the Dead where families live in five major cemeteries. Traditionally, Egyptians buried their dead in room-like "burial sites" so they could live in them during the long mourning period of forty days. Today, the population of the City of the Dead is growing rapidly because of rural migration and its complicated housing crisis that is getting worse. But the future of the City of the Dead remains uncertain. The residents of the city will not deliberately agree to relocate unless the government provides other housing for them.

In the oldest area of Cairo, there is a Coptic church, a morgue, and an old Jewish synagogue within close proximity of each other. I found it refreshing that in the devout Muslim country of Egypt there seemed to be a great deal of religious tolerance. Apparently, the Muslims, Christians, and Jews have lived here peacefully for centuries — a good role model for the rest of the world.

At the old Bazaar, I ordered a cartouche for each of my three daughters. Their names were printed in hieroglyphs onto 18K gold two-inch ovals. In ancient Egypt, kings wore cartouches to identify their royalty. A messenger delivered them to our hotel room on the last day of our trip.

The next day we flew 600 miles south of Cairo to Luxor, and boarded a yacht which was to be our home for five days as we sailed up the Nile visiting ancient temples and tombs. The temple of Luxor presides over the busiest tourist center in southern Egypt. A grand avenue lined with sphinxes once linked the temple—built by Amenhotep III (1391-1353 B.C.), and enlarged by Tutankhamen, Ramses II, and Alexander the Great —to Karnak. In 1989 a cache of more than 25 statues, many in perfect condition, was found beneath the temple courtyard.

We crossed the Nile to the Valley of the Kings which is a long dry valley or wadi running parallel to the Nile on the west bank. As we were standing in the group listening to Ahmed explaining the temple of Hatshepsut, a female pharaoh who reigned 1473-1458 B.C., I noticed a short, dark man near a donkey while tourists were taking his picture. I asked a fellow tourist to take my picture with the man and the donkey. She took two shots and went back to join the group. The man grabbed me, picked me up, and tried to put me on the donkey. I hit him several times and screamed, "Put me down!" Four big men from my group came running toward me. When the short man dropped me in the sand, I got up, kicked his shin, and ran back to my group. Ahmed talked to him and he looked frightened. Later, Ahmed told us that men with the donkeys would put a woman tourist on a donkey. The donkey would run out into the desert then the group had to pay him to go after it and return the woman. Ahmed threatened to report him to the authorities because it was illegal to harass tourists in any way. Thereafter, I stayed within my group.

We went into King Tutankhamen's tomb and Ahmed read the hieroglyphs at the entrance for us. The message was, "Who shall enter have nothing but the truth," or something awful will happen—your heart will jump out. I decided not to tell a lie while we were in the tomb; in fact I didn't talk at all. We were wearing masks because of the heavy dust. A native man walked amongst the crowd fanning the ladies to circulate the air. Each side of the gallery was covered with hieroglyphs referring to the Sphinx at Giza, the royal family, and various gods. King Tut's mummy and his treasures had been removed long ago and the tomb appeared bare. We also visited the Valley of the Queens and entered a few more tombs. My head was reeling with ancient Egyptian history. I filled a notebook with the sights I saw and later relived my trip by reading it, and looking at the many photos I took with my 35mm camera. The zoom lens afforded me some interesting shots of people without disturbing them.

We returned to our tour bus which was a large luxurious vehicle with air conditioning, comfortable seats, a refrigerator, and a small lavatory. We relaxed with a cold drink on the way back to the yacht where we had lunch and enjoyed our cruise toward Aswan. We visited several temples and tombs during the next three mornings. Our afternoons were spent on the yacht, eating, swimming in the deck pool, conversing with each other, and listening to Ahmed and John lecture on ancient Egyptian history and how it related to the Edgar Cayce Readings.

The sky was blue and clear and minarets were visible above the lush verdant palm trees. Great images of sand dunes were reflected in the smooth water of the Nile. Several birds were flying around the yacht, begging us for crumbs from our honey pastries. At sunset the glowing sun turned the whole scene into unbelievable beauty. We sat quietly, enjoying the moment and knowing we were privileged to be there.

Each day we sailed past women who were washing clothes near the bank of the river as water buffalo stood nearby munching grass. Their small homes, made of mud bricks, had no glass windows. Wooden shutters on the outside of the houses could be closed for privacy or to keep out animals. Everyone was barefooted. Children splashed water on each other as they ran and played along the shoreline. The women beat their clothes on large flat rocks, then hung them on makeshift lines to dry. As we cruised slowly past them, I felt that we were invading their privacy. They spoke to each other as they stared at us. The atmosphere was quiet, and I wondered what they thought of us. I got the impression that they didn't approve of curious tourists. They were living as their ancestors did thousands of years ago. What a diversified world! It boggled my mind to make a comparison of their life to mine.

The next morning we visited the Temple of Horus at Edfu which was built 237 B.C. to 57 B.C., into the reign of Cleopatra VII. It was built from sandstone blocks, and of all the temple remains in Egypt it is the most completely preserved. The inscriptions on its walls provide important information on language, myth, and religion during the Greco-Roman period in ancient Egypt.

In the afternoon we visited Kom Ombo to celebrate the crocodile god, Sobek. That evening after dinner, John gave a lecture on the area we had covered that day and suddenly I realized that we were in the southern part of eastern Egypt that was originally Nubia. (A thought: Did that psychic in Detroit know I would be in Nubia when she saw the letters of Nubia floating above my head? Do the Akashic Records contain information on my destiny? I was too busy to dwell on those questions at that moment.)

The next morning we docked at Aswan, which is a lively market city on the east bank of the Nile River about 80 miles south of Luxor. It is a popular tourist destination, and a launching point of many cruise ships. The Old Cataract five-star hotel sitting above the large boulders on the shoreline, with several felucca sailboats nearby bobbing in the breeze, was a scene from the movie *Death on the Nile*, an Agatha Christie mystery, starring Bette Davis, Angela Lansbury, David Niven, and Mia Farrow. I recently borrowed the DVD copy of the movie from my local library and enjoyed reliving my trip on the Nile.

It was lunch time at the Aswan market place and I chose a barbeque veggie sandwich and tea. The sauce was so spicy that my tongue tingled for an hour until I ate a honey cake. We ate as we strolled through the market examining brightly colored cotton clothing, leather sandals, crocheted beanies, straw hats, and many figurines carved from wood and marble. I bought a beanie with an ancient Nubian design and wore it the rest of the day as we visited Elephantine Island via a felucca sailboat. The boats held about ten people each and moved slowly in the warm breeze. A motorboat was available for tourists who were in a hurry.

Artifacts on the island date back to predynastic periods. Flower beds encircled the Nubian Museum, and the hollyhocks, iris, and day lilies reminded me of my own garden. Little black goats were eating the grass which eliminated the need for lawn mowers to keep the grass trim. An unfinished obelisk was nearby. We could see the Mausoleum of the Aga Kahn on the next hill. Heavy earth-moving equipment was busily digging for treasures on another nearby hill. I had the feeling that the past and the present were vying for my attention and that I was being drawn into a vortex where time stood still. A friend grabbed my arm and led me to a bench. As I sat there, eyes closed, sipping water, I wondered if I was about to have a heat stroke or if ancient memories of a previous lifetime in Nubia were being revived in my psyche. I had several dreams in which I was a dual personality, but I didn't mention them in *Following My Dreams*, because in 1981, when I wrote the book, people were less accepting of reincarnation than they are today in 2010 as I'm writing *Adventures of a Nanny*.

We took the felucca boats back to the yacht, showered, had dinner, and relaxed in the evening. The next morning we flew from Aswan to Abu Simbel to visit the great Temple of Ramses. Four seated colossi-sandstone statues of Ramses, each almost 70 feet high—front the 3,200-year-old monolith. A smaller temple celebrates his queen, glorius Nefertari, and the goddess Hathar. To save the monuments from flooding by Lake Nasser UNESCO launched a four-year salvage effort in 1964. The temple and statues were cut into 30-ton blocks and reassembled 200 feet higher up. We stood in silent awe as we stared at the beauty before us.

Returning to Cairo around 5:00 p.m, we checked-in to the Jolie Ville Airport Hotel. Our early morning flight took us non-stop to JFK in New York. From there it was a short flight to Detroit and home. I slept for twelve hours on my first night at home, then went out for a buffet of familiar American food. I hadn't eaten any meat on our trip because I didn't recognize any of the cuts. Some of the men joked about eating camel and horse roasts, so I refused all of the meat that was served. I ate the vegetables, baked goods and tea; but I lost 5 pounds during the two-week trip. Mother was feeling good and we went out to eat with friends every day for a week. It felt good to be in my home environment as I ate my way back to my normal weight.

On a sunny day in early April, Mother and I toured the garden to inspect the plants. The crocuses and snowdrops scattered shades of yellow, purple and white throughout the half-acre plot. A green haze covered various trees and shrubs, indicating that the leaf buds were opening. Shoots of daffodils, hyacinths and tulips were breaking through the soil. I held Mother's hand as we walked over the uneven ground, in awe of the signs of spring. The next day we spent hours poring over seed catalogs and planning our garden activities for the coming spring and summer. Both Mother and I enjoyed gardening; and every summer the local newspaper published colorful pictures of the beautiful flowers we grew.

In late April Mother didn't feel well and lost her appetite. I called her doctor and he gave me two prescriptions for her—which she refused to take. When she hadn't eaten for a twenty-four-hour period, I took her to the hospital emergency room where the nurse started intravenous feeding. She slept well through the night as I dozed in a chair beside her bed.

The next morning when she refused to eat her breakfast, I ate it. The nurse laughed and said she would report that to the doctor. Our neighbors took turns staying with her at the hospital. She felt better a week later although she hadn't eaten. The doctor moved her to a nearby nursing home, and two days later she had a stroke which left her comatose for several days before she died in mid-May on her eighty-fifth birthday. Friends and neighbors rallied around me and we managed to get through the unhappiness of a death in the family.

Mother had made her funeral plans ten years previously, and I worked with the funeral director to carry them out precisely as she had specified. Her beautiful multicolored tulips were blooming, and I picked a large bouquet to place on her casket. She had outlived most of her family and friends and only twenty-five people attended her funeral. Afterwards, we gathered at the Old Country Buffet, which was Mother's favorite place to eat.

I spent the next three months putting the house in order according to the city ordinance. In addition to cleaning and painting, repair work needed to be done on the fence, garage, and driveway. I donated most of the furniture and the plants in the garden to a nearby girls' school. When everything was ready, the house sold immediately, and I moved back to Arlington, VA.

ADVENTURES OF A NANNY
CHAPTER 10

To be near my daughter, Shelley, and granddaughter, Danielle, I rented a small apartment in Alexandria, VA, three miles from them, and became their number-one babysitter for a year. I had been living in the Detroit area for four years and needed to re-establish old friendships with other nannies, and get involved with A.R.E. members in the DC area. For six months I devoted much of my time to my granddaughter, attended computer and comparative religion classes at the local community college, and enjoyed not living on a tight schedule as I had done while holding down nanny jobs.

I spent many days walking the streets in Old Town Alexandria absorbing the early American atmosphere, imagining I'd lived there in the George Washington era. I enjoyed visiting the Torpedo Factory Art Center and observing artists at their craftwork. Nationally recognized for its early American architecture, variety of hotels, unique boutiques, award-winning restaurants and inexpensive historic attractions—as well as quick and easy access to the many free Washington, DC sites— Alexandria is the perfect getaway to shop, dine, and celebrate. The bus tours from Alexandria to George Washington's Historic Mount Vernon Estate and Gardens offer fascinating data on everyday life in northern Virginia and the DC area during the formation of our country.

I reconnected with ADCAN (the nanny association in DC), and was delighted to see former nanny friends and their little charges who had grown considerably while I'd been in Detroit. I accompanied a group of them on an outing to the National Zoo in DC. The children were wide-eyed as they observed the elephants, giraffes, monkeys, bears, and many other animals; but their favorite animal was the baby panda. We sat on benches and watched intently as the pandas devoured bamboo shoots and interacted with each other. After lunch at a hot dog stand the children were sleepy and we headed for home.

My idyllic situation ended abruptly when my landlord posted a notice on my front door which stated that all tenants must move within thirty days because the building had been sold and would be renovated into business offices. My lease was up in thirty days, so I had no recourse but to call the nanny employment agency and find an apartment and job combination posthaste.

I interviewed with three new moms and chose to live with a couple in their mid-thirties who were computer scientists, that had immigrated from India ten years previously. Mom had taken a six-month maternity leave and was now ready to go back to work. I moved into their home in Reston, VA (about forty-five minutes from downtown DC) and we started to settle into a routine. Little three-month-old Rajah was a sweet, placid baby, and we thought he was adjusting to his new feeding schedule (Mom was weaning him onto a baby formula), when after two weeks of rescheduling his life he became ill, vomiting and crying incessantly. He was admitted to the hospital for a week where it was determined he was severely allergic to the baby formula and other foods. That necessitated Mom to continue nursing him every three hours during the daytime, and whenever he awoke at night. Mom, Dad, and I were very upset, to say the least. Mom confided to me that she couldn't afford to pay me unless she went back to her job. I told her I would stay and help her without pay for a few weeks and hopefully, baby Raja would improve. She was relieved and grateful for my offer.

I stayed with them for six weeks while Raja steadily improved. Mom decided to postpone going back to work so she could take care of Rajah without help. In the meantime she taught me to cook vegetarian meals. I loved exploring the tasty spices and new methods for food preparation. Dad appreciated the food and took leftovers to work for his lunch. We cooked every day and Dad gained six pounds while I was there. He needed the extra weight and looked healthy. He was helpful with Raja and household chores, and I knew they could take care of themselves without my help, so I called the nanny agency looking for a new adventure.

Out of several good job offers, I chose three-month-old Jonathon whose mom was going back to work after a six-month maternity leave. Baby Jonathon was thriving on his formula and everybody was happy. Mom and Dad were lawyers with offices in downtown DC. Their home was located in McLean, VA near the CIA Headquarters. Mom took me for a drive through the neighborhood, pointing out the shopping area, and houses where well-known people lived. The estate where the Robert Kennedys had lived looked lonely with the empty playground. Their children had grown up and moved away. When my own children grew up I became a preschool teacher and nanny so I could be with children. I think that is my life's purpose, and parents and kids are happy with my loving attention.

My new apartment was in the attic of a large English Tudor house, with lots of sunshine streaming through the windows. Dad helped me carry my luggage upstairs and I unpacked and settled in to live with a happy, perpetually smiling baby boy whose hair was a mass of golden curls. His blue eyes sparkled when he looked at me and we fell in love immediately.

On Mom's first day back in her office she called me three times to check on Jonathon. I assured her that he was all right and that he was lying on a blanket on the floor doing the dog paddle while perched on his tummy. I laughed at his baby antics several times a day and was delighted to be his nanny. He stayed on his feeding schedule and never cried, slept through the night without disturbing his parents, enjoyed his bath, and we lived in a happy household.

One day Jonathon and I were out strolling in the neighborhood and met a nanny whom I hadn't seen in three years. I was surprised to learn that she had married the brother of a former employer and had her own one-year-old baby. She managed her own interior decorating business and had a nanny for her baby. I felt that she was missing the pleasure of caring for her own baby, but she seemed to be happy with her situation and I didn't criticize her. We met twice a week, strolled the babies and had coffee with a nanny/baby group at a nearby park.

When Jonathon was one year old, Mom's cousin died unexpectedly of a heart attack. Mom and Dad flew to Los Angeles for the funeral then continued on to Hawaii for a much needed respite. I invited my cousin Lee in Coalwood, WV to stay with me for two weeks and Jonathon and I picked her up at Dulles Airport. We had a great time catching up on family news and playing with

Jonathon. Lee told me about a movie, *October Sky*, which was adapted from *Rocket Boys: A Memoir,* a book by Homer Hickam, a native of Coalwood. I lived in Coalwood for a year when I was a child but I didn't know him. We rented the movie from the video store and watched it with much enthusiasm. I bought the book the following week and enjoyed reading about places in Coalwood that were familiar to me. Later, I read all of Homer's books. (See Homer Hickam.com)

Lee and I had two weeks to have fun! I took her on a tour of DC. We visited the Washington Monument, the Lincoln Memorial, and the National Zoo in one day. Jonathon was happy in his stroller with his binky and bottle and fell asleep on the way home. The next day we shopped at Tysons Corner, buying new clothes for Lee. We rested one day at home then drove down I-95 and spent one day and night in Fredricksburg, VA. We drove to Williamsburg, VA for a day and night, then continued south to Virginia Beach for a beautiful weekend by the ocean. I met with a group of old friends for dinner while Lee kept Jonathon at the hotel. He was a happy camper, a real fun baby.

Back home in McLean, we decided to go to a lecture by Carol Ann Liaros at the Unity Church in Oakton, VA. I put Jonathon in the church nursery where the kids were having a great time and Lee and I went into the auditorium. I had met Carol Ann previously and read her book, *Intuition Made Easy*. She greeted me with: "Well, well, look who's here, the healer from Egypt!" I introduced her to Lee whose facial expression exhibited resigned skepticism as we passed by in a long line of well-wishers. Carol Ann's book was already a big seller. As we took our seats, Lee whispered, "How did she know you went to Egypt?" I answered, "She's a mind reader." Lee replied, "Don't josh me."

The next day I convinced Lee to get a reading from my friend, Lloyd, who reads the Akashic Records. I'd had three one-hour readings from him, asking a total of forty questions which he had answered with precise information on tape. I dropped her off at Lloyd's house one evening while I went grocery shopping with Jonathon. When I picked her up an hour later, she said her head was reeling with information he had given her from "outer space." I listened to her taped reading while we stayed up late that night. She talked incessantly about her "unusual experience." During the twenty years that I'd read books about Edgar Cayce and other psychics I'd had my own "unusual experiences," and I knew what she was feeling.

We spent several hours at Mount Vernon in Alexandria on a sunny afternoon, then we relaxed and conversed for a couple of days before Mom and Dad returned home.

Jonathon was delighted to see his parents who had planned to spend the weekend with him before returning to work. Lee and I went to Dulles Airport and boarded a small plane with six passengers for Bluefield, WV at 5:45 p.m. I didn't mind a two-hour flight, but I was a little apprehensive when the pilot emerged from the cockpit and asked a heavy man on the left side of the plane to change seats with a small woman on the right side in order to more evenly distribute the weight in the plane. The plane's motor was noisy and we had to speak loudly to each other to be heard. When we finally got to bed that night we slept soundly.

Visiting with my relatives was fun and feasting time. They roared at Lee's explanation of her psychic reading and took it with a grain of salt. We were good-time revelers. Lee and I visited the launch-pad site that Homer Hickam and the Rocket Boys built. There were several tourists there from London and Wales. Of course, *October Sky* (book and movie) had fans worldwide who came to Coalwood for the Rocket Boys Festival in October (see Coalwoodmemories.com).

Time goes fast when we're having fun and we had to leave for the airport at 9 a.m. the next morning. Lee planned to fly back to Dulles with me, then fly to Sarasota, FL to visit her son. We boarded the same plane we had arrived on, but the pilot didn't rearrange any

passengers. The airport was located on the top of a
mountain. As we taxied down the runway we didn't go up;
instead, we ran off the end of the runway and went down,
barely missing the tree tops, before the plane started to
climb. I had the heebie-jeebies all the way back to Dulles.
About midnight as I slept, lightning struck a tree just
outside my bedroom window leaving a large burned spot
about six feet up from the roots. Needless to say, my sleep
was ruined for that night.

The following day, while Jonathon was taking a
nap, I lay on the couch watching *Cold Case Files* on TV
when the doorbell startled me as it buzzed repeatedly
while the bad guy on the show was hitting a woman. I was
afraid to go to the door. I peeked from behind a drapery

and saw a delivery man from the florist shop getting into a van. At that moment my phone rang; it was the delivery man. I opened the door and told him I was afraid to answer the door because the TV show scared me. He said, "That's okay, I wouldn't open the door, either, for someone who looks like me." I laughed, and happily received flowers from my daughter for my birthday.

Mom and Dad wanted a getaway weekend in Berkeley Springs, WV and asked me to go along to take care of Jonathon. We were all in a good mood as we headed west on Route 7 toward West Virginia's Eastern Panhandle, approximately ninety minutes from home. For more than two centuries, folks have traveled to the tiny mountain town of Berkeley Springs to enjoy the warm mineral water and to relax in the quiet atmosphere as they hike, play golf and tennis, and breathe the fresh mountain air. George Washington and other Founding Fathers established the country's first spa at Berkeley Springs in 1776.

Jonathon sat in his car seat alternating between his binky and sippy cup while we looked at picture books. He was a contended baby and I adored him.

Mom had three spa appointments on Saturday and Jonathon and I strolled the grounds and chatted with others who were there relaxing. There were no cars nearby and the stillness was soothing as I rocked him to sleep on the big front porch of the inn. Mom and Dad's room was about fifty feet down the hall from the room I shared with Jonathon, which did not have a private bath. He looked puzzled when I placed his portable potty beside his bed instead of in the bathroom. However, he never complained and enjoyed whatever we were doing.

We got up at 6 a.m. and went downstairs for breakfast. Only moms or nannies with small children were in the restaurant. We had pancakes and scrambled eggs. Jonathon usually ate whatever we put on the table in front of him. Afterwards we went for a leisurely walk around the grounds, then read picture books in a rocker on the front porch, while waiting for Mom and Dad to make an appearance. They liked to sleep late so we didn't disturb them. I look back on that weekend as the calm before the storm.

A few days later Mom left for her office in downtown DC and Dad and I took Jonathon to his first day of nursery school. Jonathon didn't like being in the room with fifteen other two-year olds. The noisy crowd confined us to miniature chairs at a corner table, where we observed the confusion as Jonathon held my hand in a tight grip. He started crying and a teacher picked him up, said a few soothing words to him, and asked us to leave.

She said he would be okay. Other parents and nannies were leaving also.

As we descended the front steps, a man came running toward us shouting, "They're bombing New York—get your kids and go home and watch TV!" Of course we were stunned. The date was 9/11/01 which everyone would forever remember. We ran back inside the nursery, picked up Jonathon and headed for home.

Dad ran for the TV, grabbing the ringing phone, speaking to Mom, who was frantic. She informed us that she couldn't come home because all traffic was halted at the Beltway, and she would stay at a friend's house in DC temporarily. I took Jonathon into an adjoining room and started a Sesame Street video for him. I didn't want him to see the horror we were watching on TV. I answered the doorbell to see a terrified nanny friend with her one-year-old charge, who lived about a mile from the Pentagon. When she heard the explosion of the plane crash and saw black smoke rising from the Pentagon, she grabbed the toddler and came to our house. The baby's parents were out of town and I assured her she could stay overnight with me. Several neighbors had gathered at our house trying to comfort each other. We had plenty of food on hand due to my shopping spree the previous day, so I fired up the outside grill and started to cook. My hands were shaking and my knees felt week as I tried to evaluate the devastation that had happened to our country that morning. That afternoon American flags were raised all over the neighborhood. Mom stayed overnight with her friend and told us of her plans for Jonathon the next day. She was going to put him in a day care center in her office building. She would be able to see him during the day, and he would ride with his parents to work and back everyday. I had been his nanny from age three months to almost three years and we were very much attached to each other. It was time for him to socialize with other children and the day care situation seemed to provide all of his needs, including more time with his Mom and Dad. I offered to stay for a month after he started the new routine and keep out of sight so he could better adjust to the new people in his life. He got along great with everyone, and I started a new job in Great Falls, VA.

November 15, 2001

To Whom It May Concern:

Rachel Kendal has a true love of children. Her patience, experience, and confidence are extremely trustworthy. She makes a point of being clear in communicating her recommendations, processes, procedures, and her "child first" interest.

Other than ourselves (parents), we could not have had a better person care for our child. Rachel was the right person for our home and she has become part of our family. She's wonderful!

Mom in McLean, VA

ADVENTURES OF A NANNY

CHAPTER 11

In April 2002 I went to interview with a single mom and her two young sons. Big brother Kirk was three years old, a handsome boy with dark hair and hazel eyes, and baby William was eight months old with sky-blue eyes and dark hair. It was delightful just to look at him. They sat on the floor, engrossed in picture books while Mom and I talked. The boy's grandmother had always been their caregiver, but now she was having health problems and needed to retire.

Mom said she had interviewed several nannies, but hadn't found one that seemed right for her boys. After two hours of playing with the boys and some serious conversation with Mom, she asked me to be their nanny. I accepted the invitation and the following weekend I moved into their townhouse in Vienna, VA and started a six-year adventure with two fun boys.

Of course, I encountered a few minor problems the first week while getting acquainted with the household routine. Kirk attended preschool five days a week, which necessitated that I use all of my early-morning energy to get them ready to leave the house by 9 a.m. After dropping Kirk off and assuring him that Mom would pick him up at 6 p.m., William and I went grocery shopping. He fell asleep on the way home and I carried him up the three-story townhouse (thirty-six steps) to his bedroom. Two hours later I carried him downstairs, gave him a snack and we read a picture book. He was beginning to talk and identified some of the animal pictures. While he watched Sesame Street, I began to scout around the main floor and to figure out a better way to organize the house to accommodate two small boys and myself with the least physical effort on my part. After Mom approved my plans, I bought the necessary equipment to make the living-dining-kitchen area safe for a crawling baby. I installed three folding gates to stairways leading into the living room so baby Will could crawl everywhere. I also installed aluminum bars on the bottom of the large front window so he could pull himself up and look out of the window which was directly above the concrete entrance to the underground garage. I also installed bars on the top floor bedroom windows. In my opinion these were child-safe issues that should be addressed by every household involving children. However, when Dad came to pick up the boys for a visit, he raved and ranted, referring to the house as looking like a jail. Needless to say, he did not win me over. During the six years I was there, we locked horns repeatedly. Mom's standing order to me was: "Take care of the boys in any way you see fit." She was relieved to follow my lead in childcare since she had no experience with her boys because Grandmother had raised them so far. Dad knew nothing of childcare, but was fighting her in court to get custody of them.

So, I was subpoenaed to court along with the boys' grandmother because Dad accused us of being inept in childcare. He maintained that his mother would come to live with him and the boys and provide a better home environment for them in Arizona where he was going to intern at a hospital. A female judge sat on the bench and looked at all of us with disfavor. The bailiff, who was about 6' 5", 250 pounds, did not look friendly.

All eyes watched Mom as she sashayed down the aisle and took a seat at the front of the room. Her shoulder-length red hair, green dress, and high-heel shoes that made her six-feet tall, belied the fact that she was a very competent business lawyer.

Dad, who had just finished medical school, was wearing dirty jeans, a T-shirt, and a ponytail halfway down his back. He was slightly smaller than the bailiff, who looked at him with disdain. When he was called to the stand, his demeanor was loud and confrontational, causing the judge to say, "Quiet in the courtroom!" He stated his complaints about Grandmother and me. Actually, he knew nothing about our caregiving abilities because we had not all been present when the boys were going through their daily routines. In essence, he was just lying. His lawyer encouraged him to keep giving defamatory statements.

Next, Dad's lawyer put Grandmother on the stand; and she wasn't one to mince words as he questioned her about her style of childcare. Dad had accused her of not feeding Kirk nutritious food.

Lawyer: "Please tell the court what Kirk eats for breakfast."

Grandmother: "He usually eats whole grain cereal or toast, a glass of milk and fruit."

Lawyer: "What does he eat for lunch?"

Grandmother: "He usually eats a peanut butter sandwich, milk, and fruit."

Lawyer: "What does he eat for dinner?"

Grandmother: "I give him raw vegetables, a hot dog, and milk."

Lawyer: "Why don't you give him meat?"

Grandmother: "He eats hot dogs."

Lawyer raising his voice: "Do you call a hot dog meat?"

Grandmother: "Well, it's not a vegetable."

The laughter in the courtroom angered the judge and she, again, called for order. When I took the stand,

Dad's lawyer tried to frustrate me by asking unnecessary questions.

Lawyer: "How much is your salary:"

Rachel: "$600 per week."

Lawyer: "How much is that per hour?"

Judge: "Strike that question."

Lawyer: "Do you get free room and board and a car at your disposal?"

Rachel: "Yes."

Lawyer: "How much is that worth?"

Judge: "Strike that question."

Lawyer: "What makes you think you're qualified to care for Kirk and William?"

Rachel: "After twenty years of caring for my own three children I graduated from the University of Michigan with a bachelor's degree in child development and psychology. I've been a preschool teacher and nanny for over twenty years."

Lawyer: "No more questions."

The judge called for a half-hour recess, and when we convened she said the boys were to stay with their mother and their competent nanny. Dad jumped up from his chair and ran toward Mom. Two bailiffs grabbed him, pushed him down into a chair, and pinned him between them where he could see their guns. It was quite an ordeal for a nanny. Little did I know what was brewing in his belligerent head; but I found out as the next six years unfolded.

Mom, Grandmother, and I went home, picked up the boys, and took them out to dinner. Yes, Kirk ordered a hot dog, and we celebrated with steaks. We knew that Dad would soon be in Arizona and too far away to fulfill his alloted time with the boys, which was Wednesday evening visits and every other weekend at his home. We felt free!

While Will took his morning nap, I took the laundry to the first level of the townhouse where the washer and dryer were located in the closet near the boys' playroom. As I was putting clothes into the washer I noticed food stains on the front of my blouse and jeans. I took them off and put them in the washer. Toys were strewn all over the play area and I started picking them up. I couldn't carry them all, so I put the football helmet on my head and held the football under my arm. As I walked toward the toy bin, I looked down the hall and saw that the garage door was open and a man was reading the gas meter just outside the garage. He turned around and saw me, looked me over and laughed uproariously. I was scared, embarrassed, and angry, all at once. As I ran up the steps, I heard him holler, "I hope your team wins, lady."

I hurriedly got dressed, took Will out of his crib and we went into the kitchen for lunch. He was such a beautiful baby and I adored him. He had a good appetite and drank milk from a bottle. His pediatrician had recommended that Mom nurse him until he was one year old. So, as soon as she got home from work Will nursed for ten minutes. He usually stood by the window and watched for her to return, holding a binky in his mouth and one in each hand. I kept a fresh supply of binkys in a kitchen drawer because I couldn't stand to see a baby crying for a lost binky.

I decreased Kirk's time at preschool to 9:30 a.m. to 3 p.m., three days a week. I wanted him to bond with Will and me. I felt that the boys didn't have enough time together when Kirk was at preschool five days a week on his previous schedule. We went to the park almost every afternoon and met other children and their moms and nannies. Will didn't walk by himself until he was fourteen months old, but he crawled up steps instead of being carried. When he finally got his equilibrium for walking, he never stopped running. He was very talkative and delightful to care for. Kirk was a bookworm. As I read to him with my finger tracing each sentence he learned to read. As he approached his fourth birthday, he was reading the books to Will and teaching him the alphabet.

Kirk told me that he had married Zoee, one of his classmates. I thought that was cute and I told his teacher.

She replied, "That's great, but what will his other five wives say?" He was popular with the girls.

We were busy and the months passed by quickly. In October we raked leaves and stored the patio furniture and outside toys in the garage. During the winter we played in the snow and had a great Christmas celebration. In the following spring when Will was twenty-two months old we were getting the patio area ready for outdoor play. Will picked up a set of wind chimes, walked over to the tree where they had hung previously and said, "This goes up there." I was stunned to realize he had remembered me taking them down the previous October when we took the patio furniture inside. I get excited when I discover a child who is exceptionally bright. I want to stuff their brains full of information that will help them to have a happy life. I knew that I had two little boys who were eager to learn, and I was going to enjoy infusing more knowledge into their developing intellect.

They made me laugh every day with their child-like reasoning. Will was beginning to wear underwear instead of diapers. I gave him some new boys' briefs and he put them on. Even though Elmo and the Cookie Monster smiled at us from his backside, he said he didn't like them. He said, "They're too tight. This hurts my leg. It's too tight on my belly button. I'm choking." We laughed at him and handed him a diaper which he donned with his pajamas, and we went outside on the deck to look at the stars through a telescope. I said to Will, "Look, there's a half-moon." He said, "Where's the other half?" I said, "Believe it or not, it's up there." He said, "I don't believe it."

Kirk was showing a good sense of humor with the knock-knock jokes he picked up at preschool. One day he said to me, "Rachel, will you always remember me?" I said, "Sure." He said, "Knock-knock." I said, "Who's there?" He said, "You forgot me already."

I picked up the phone one afternoon and heard Pierre say, "Rachel, how soon can you get ready to come to Paris?" I said, "Real soon—like fifteen minutes!" Pierre, who lived in Paris, was a close friend to Mom's family. As a lawyer and very successful businessman who traveled the world, he had been a great comfort to Mom while she was going through the trials and tribulations of the divorce procedure. For three months he lived at a nearby hotel, and we consulted him almost daily on legal matters. The boys adored him, and he wanted us to spend two weeks with him at his home in Paris. We were elated!

A week later, the four of us were in a stretch limo with six pieces of luggage, on our way to Dulles Airport to board a plane for the overnight flight to Charles de Gaulle Airport in Paris. When we arrived, Pierre was waiting for us with hugs and kisses, and another stretch limo. We went to his home near the Notre Dame Cathedral and ate a delicious meal that his maid had prepared for us. The boys and I went outside to explore the garden and walled area that ensured the privacy of the estate. Mom and Pierre perused legal documents pertaining to her divorce.

The next day jet lag caught up with me and I stayed home napping while Pierre and Mom took the boys to Disneyland. We went to a nearby restaurant for dinner and returned home to watch TV and relax. Since the boys and I couldn't understand the French language, Mom and Pierre explained the movie's plot to us. We stayed in Paris for four days, pushing the boys in strollers as we explored the beautiful city. However, to my dismay, we could not get into the Louvre museum due to the large crowd. I wondered if I'd ever get to see the Mona Lisa.

We ate at sidewalk cafes, leaving crumbs everywhere, and the pigeons were grateful. Will took naps in his stroller and never complained. We boarded a boat for a cruise along the Seine River. An audio announcement system synchronized to the boat's movement provided commentary on the passing sights and some of the city's oldest and most majestic historic monuments. There were legendary surprises at every turn—from the grand Notre Dame Cathedral to the iconic Eiffel Tower.

At the high-speed French Railway System we boarded a train for Saint-Remy-de-Provence where Pierre had a smaller home that he used when he was in the south of France. We enjoyed the trip as we gazed at the beautiful fields of sunflowers and lavender, seemingly growing unattended between small villages. We passed by the Pont du Gard, a 150-feet high Roman aqueduct, a mere two-thousand years old. The Provence countryside was a blend of medieval walled towers, farms, mountains, and charming villages.

Pierre's friend met us at the train station with two cars to take us to his home in Saint-Remy. The village of Saint-Remy is pretty and picturesque, and the old Gallo-Roman interior is encircled by the remnants of the circular 14th century wall and the protective circle of buildings.

Located on the plains at the northern edge of the Alpilles, 20 km south of Avignon, this is where Van Gogh painted Starry Night, Nostradamus was born and Dr. Albert Schweitzer was a prisoner. Walking down Rue Nostradamus, we found the Nostradamus fountain where I took the boys' picture. Saint-Remy is a busy, active village, with a good selection of restaurants and hotels for the traveler. Among the shops in the old village are a few with some regional pottery, including some beautiful sunflower plates no doubt influenced by Van Gogh.

We stayed in Saint-Remy for three days, participating in the street festivals and visiting the Roman ruins. The boys climbed on stone mausoleums, triumphal arches, statues of Roman citizenry, and fallen columns of ancient buildings. Needless to say, they had scratched arms and legs which I treated with antiseptic cream.

The five of us headed for Marseille and the Mediterranean Sea. A port city, Marseille is known to be more than 2,600 years old, since prehistoric wall paintings were recently discovered in a cave of the Calanques creeks. It was incorporated into the kingdom of France in 1981. The 19th century propelled Marseille into modern times.

After lunch at a sidewalk cafe, we walked on the beach where most of us were wearing sweaters in the 60° mid-October weather. My memory wandered back to an old 1944 movie I saw titled *Passage To Marseille* with Humphrey Bogart. I wondered if they had actually shot any of it in Marseille. I felt at peace holding Will's hand as we walked, crunching sand under our feet. I was in awe as I looked out over the Mediterranean Sea and the azure sky, thinking: What a beautiful world! My reverie was interrupted as Will pulled his hand from mine and ran toward the Sea. I chased him and grabbed his arm just before he stepped into the surf.

We returned to Paris and took the boys to play in the park near the French Parliament building. Pierre told me he wanted to have a personal conversation with me so Mom and the boys went to the other side of the park. The gist of the conversation was that he wanted to marry Mom and have me live with the family in Paris. I was stunned, but gladly accepted the offer because my youngest daughter, Shelley, was living in Milan, Italy with her Italian husband, and Pierre assured me it was only a short flight away from Paris. However, there were gigantic obstacles to overcome: He hadn't asked Mom yet; permission from the court was mandatory for the boys to leave the United States; and their dad opposed everything Mom wanted to do pertaining to their welfare, just for spite; the boys and I would have to learn to speak French; and it would mean giving up our familiar lifestyle for one that was totally different.

Mom and the boys were swinging high on the playground when we joined them, and we all went for hot chocolate at the refreshment stand. Later that evening I heard raised voices coming from upstairs as I was

watching the boys play in the basement hot tub. I surmised that Mom had said "no" to his proposal and refused the $20,000 engagement ring that he had showed me in the park. I tucked the boys into their beds and didn't speak to Mom until the next morning as we packed to go home. Pierre ordered two taxis for us, kissed the boys and me—avoiding Mom, and didn't go to the train station with us. I felt sad and confused but kept up the happy chatter with the boys.

We needed a few days to settle back into our household routine. I didn't mention Pierre to Mom or the boys. A week later Mom told me that she wouldn't give up her career for anybody; that she intended to live her life on her own terms. I said, "Right on!" I knew of two other lawyers who were hot on her trail for marriage, but her divorce was not final, and she just wanted to be free. I'm divorced and I know that great feeling of freedom.

When Will was barely three years old he could recite the alphabet, count to 50, print his name, and spell three-letter words. He seldom made a mistake and Kirk was always ready to correct him. One day while we were eating lunch, Will ran from the table and said, "I need to go poopy—p-o-o-p-e." Kirk ran after him yelling the correct spelling.

Kirk was excited about going to kindergarten at a nearby public school. On the first day the three of us walked to school and started looking for Kirk's classroom. As we entered a long hallway, we heard a child screaming and crying. Several moms, nannies, and kids watched transfixed as two teachers carried a second grade boy toward the principal's office. One teacher was gripping his ankles, and the other pinned his arms to his chest as they carried him. No one said a word as we backed against the wall to let them pass by. Later, Mom and I laughed as the boys told her the "horrific" story. We never had a bad report about them from their teachers. They got the message.

Will started preschool three mornings per week and I picked him up at 1 p.m. after he ate lunch with the other students. We usually shopped before going home and one day he asked me to stop at the Mattress Warehouse. I said, "Why?" He said, "I want to jump on the beds." I said, "Not a chance." When we got home we watched Bert and Ernie, and relaxed until Kirk came home. The nanny next door had a boy in Kirk's class and we took turns walking them to school.

Mostly, the following year was a calm routine of school for the boys with plenty of fun activities and only two visits from Dad who was doing an internship in Arizona. He called the boys every other week, and sent them presents. However, he was still angry at Mom and sent her email almost daily to aggravate her. Sometimes she got very upset with him and asked me to help her reply to his obstinate behavior. After a few chosen words from me, he would let up for a week or so.

Mom had other problems to settle. She was engaged to a man she met on the Internet, and didn't trust him. I didn't like him because he lied about his financial affairs and she realized she would be losing a lot of money if they each sold their homes and bought a large home together. He had two boys who lived with him, and a male nanny. The problem was solved one day when she saw his advertisement seeking a girlfriend on the Internet. I never saw him again.

The boys liked to talk about food at mealtime. They sat on stools at the kitchen counter and watched as I prepared their meals or mixed ingredients for baking. As I started to bake cookies one day, Will mounted a stool and said, "Rachel, do you know what French fries are made out of?"

"What?"

"They're made out of French toast."

That's four-year-old logic. He continued the conversation.

"Are McDonald's chicken nuggets real chicken?"

"Yes, but the chicken nuggets we have at home are soy."

"Ugh! Are hot dogs really dogs?"

"No."

"What are they made of?"

"A soy product."

"Oh."

I couldn't tell him people eat animals or he wouldn't eat meat with Mom and Grandmother. The boys and I ate soy products daily, such as soy burgers, sausage, soy milk, chicken nuggets, and cheese. We especially liked soy sausage crumbled on pizza. They liked to place the toppings on pizza and set the oven temperature.

Kirk joined us and read the directions on the cookie-mix box. When he read "mix by hand," he ran around the counter and stuck his hand in the wet ingredients. I grabbed his hand, rinsed it under the sink faucet, and explained to him that "mix by hand" also meant using a spoon instead of an electric mixer. I picked up a sponge, wiped the counter, rinsed it, put it in the microwave oven and pressed 15 seconds to sanitize it. Will said, "Rachel, why are you cooking a sponge?" (More four-year-old logic) My mantra at that moment was, Ohm—Ohmm—Ohmmm.

While the cookies were baking we sat at the counter and continued our conversation. Will was learning "jokes" at preschool and told them to us. He started with:

"What do you call a cow that eats grass?"

"What?"

"A lawn mooer."

"What's worse than finding a worm in an apple?"

"What?"

"Finding half a worm."

"Knock, knock."

"Who's there?"

"Police."

"Police who?"

"Police let me in—it's cold out here."

I congratulated Will on the math paper he brought home from school and said, "How do you know the answers?" He said, "I either count in my head or on my fingers."

Will: "Rachel, what is a mother tongue?"
Kirk: "That's when your mother hollers at you."
Rachel: "That's a person's native language."

Just then Mom arrived from work and the boys pounced on her with kisses. She grabbed a cookie, started upstairs, and said, "Come on, boys. It's shower time."

Kirk: "I don't know why I always have to take a shower."

Rachel: "Because you're always dirty. I don't know what we're going to do with you."

Mom: "Let's use a scrub brush on him."

The next afternoon I told the boys I was going to cut their hair. Of course, they said, "Oh no!" because they would have to sit still for twenty minutes each. However, I assembled the scissors, electric clippers, comb, and a spray bottle of water, and placed them on a kitchen counter. Kirk was first to sit on the kitchen stool facing the TV for entertainment while getting a haircut. He started a conversation with:

"I think I've got lice."
Rachel: "What?"

Kirk: "My hair sticks straight up and they're running all over my head."

I said a silent prayer, then examined his hair. Thankfully, I found no lice, and I gave him a GI haircut to eliminate hiding places for lice. He liked the short hair and said, "Now, I don't have to comb my hair." No subject was off-limits at hair-cutting time, so he started asking questions.

Kirk: "Do you need a passport to go to New Mexico?"

Rachel: "No, New Mexico is one of the United States of America."

Kirk: "Are we Homo sapiens?"

Rachel: "Yes."

Kirk: "Yuk."

Rachel: "Your innate intelligence is lying dormant in you today."

Kirk: "What?"

Rachel: "Go watch TV while I cut your brother's hair."

Will climbed up onto the stool and started describing the wrestling match he had with Kirk the previous day. He said Kirk got a hammerlock on him, threw him on the floor and sat on his stomach while choking him. I called for Kirk to listen to Will's accusation against him. Kirk admitted it was true, but called Will a baby and said he was only playing.

I grabbed Kirk in a hammerlock, placed him on the floor face down, straddled his body, and asked him if we were just playing. He was completely taken aback. I said, "Now you know how Will felt when you attacked him." He apologized to Will and went back to the TV program. Will was elated with the demonstration and bent over giggling. I said, "You better sit still or you will wind up looking like Dr. Phil."

For Easter vacation, we rented a condo in Sarasota, FL at Siesta Key beach for two weeks. Grandmother went with us and we had a great time. My daughter, Debra, lived in Sarasota and spent time with us. She took us to the aquarium where the boys were delighted to pet the stingrays whose stingers had been removed. Several children around a circular tank fed the stingrays and stroked their backs. I silently said, "yuk," and led the boys to a sink to wash their hands. The next day, I said "yuk" again when Will showed me a handfull of tiny, crushed crabs that he had dug out of the sand while playing on the beach. I was glad to see nearby sandpipers eating the crabs before Will could get more of them.

The boys had been taking piano lessons for a year and Will really enjoyed playing; but Kirk was less enthusiastic and had to be told when to practice. Luckily, the condo had a piano and the boys played at least a half hour every day. Kirk was at the piano one day, trying my patience, and I finally said, "Stop it! That's annoying. You're not making music. You're making a pest of yourself." He said, "I can't find my lesson book." I said, "Play it by ear." He seriously said, "I can't play the piano with my ear." We burst into laughter. I could see that we were beyond the realm of reasoning for the afternoon, and Grandmother offered to take them shopping for new sandals and ice cream. While they were gone for two hours I took a break under a palm tree with ice-cold tea and *Revelation*, a commentary based on a study of twenty-three discourses by Edgar Cayce, which helped me to better understand the *Book of Revelation* in the Bible.

Kirk was scheduled to make his first Holy Communion at St. Mark's Catholic Church with two hundred other children the following year, and Grandmother and I were helping him with his catechism lessons. The boys listened intently when I talked about God and religious dogma, and asked questions that I couldn't always answer. They were especially interested in heaven since Buzz Aldrin had visited their school and talked to the children about outer space. They wore T-shirts with ALDRIN across their chest. Kirk wanted to know why he couldn't go to heaven in a rocket and eliminate his religious studies. I pointed my left index finger straight up above my head which indicated that God was watching his behavior. He settled down with a "joke." Kirk: "What did one wall say to another?" Rachel: "What?" Kirk: "Meet you in the corner."

We enjoyed our time at the beach, and Debra drove the boys and me to the airport while Mom, Grandmother, and the luggage went in a taxi. We arrived at Dulles Airport at 7 p.m. which was almost bedtime for the boys. After milk and crackers, they fell asleep. They had to go to school the next morning.

As the boys ate breakfast at the counter, watching me pack their lunches, I asked, "What would you like for lunch today?" Kirk said, "What's on the menu?" I named every morsel of food in the house, including the contents of the flour bin and he said, "Is that all?"

I took them to school and then shopped for food. Will's piano teacher called me and said he's the most advanced five-year-old student she's ever had in her class. I informed her that he had been taking piano lessons for a year and really loved the piano. Will beamed that evening at the dinner table when I told everyone of the teacher's comments. When Dad called, Will played the piano over the phone for him, and later he whispered to me, "Rachel, I missed a note." I said, "That's okay. We didn't notice. To us, you're another Liberace."

Will: "Something awful happened at school today."

Rachel: "What happened?"

Will: "Fairfax County banned Little Debbie snack cakes from the cafeteria. They said kids are eating too much sugar."

Rachel: "Put some wheat crackers in your backpack for tomorrow's snack."

Will: "Kirk's looking at me and laughing."

Rachel: "Tell him 'ditto'."

Will: "What does that mean?"

Rachel: "The same back to you, brother. Now, stop the grouching or you'll be a grandpa before you're six years old."

Kirk laughed, and I told him to go to the piano and practice. He grouched and I said, "You seem to be affected by extreme inertia when it's time to practice your piano lesson—just do it!"

That weekend we went to the Theater-in-the-Woods at Wolf Trap Farm Park and sat on benches outside while we watched children perform various acts of singing, dancing, and humorous skits. After lunch on Saturday, we shopped for summer clothes at Tysons Corner. They had outgrown their clothes from the previous summer and were eager to get new outfits. As we walked through Nordstrom's toddlers' department, Will saw a small stuffed bear and said, "I want that." I said, "No, that's for babies. You're a big boy now." He said, "When I come back as a baby, can I have it?" I was stunned to realize that he understood the theory of reincarnation. Apparently, he had been listening when Kirk and I were discussing concepts in his religious studies preparing him for his First Holy Communion. Wonders will never cease when you're working with children.

For several years, I had hoarded my frequent-flyer miles and now I wanted to use them for a fun trip with the boys. Mom and I planned a trip to the Grand Canyon, and two weeks later we were sitting in Dulles Airport waiting for our plane to Phoenix, AZ. I went to get coffee and when I returned five minutes later the boys were nowhere in sight. Mom said they went to the men's room. Apparently she didn't know that pedophiles hang out in men's rooms. I ran across the waiting area and opened the door to the men's room hollering, "Kirk and Will, come here now!" They emerged from a stall with quizzical looks at me. I didn't see anyone else in the room, and I told them to wash their hands while I stood in the doorway. I think normal behavior for a mom or nanny is to always be alert to the possibilities of a child getting in harm's way.

When we arrived in Phoenix we rented a car and drove to Williams in about two hours, where we got a room at a lodge. We stayed there for two nights, then boarded a 19th century train for the South Rim of the Grand Canyon where we stayed in a cabin for two nights while we observed, in awe, the beautiful Canyon. As we boarded a helicopter to fly over the Canyon, I said to the pilot: "When did you learn to fly a helicopter?" He answered: "When I was a medic in Vietnam." I said: "Okay, let's go." We got a clear view of the Supai village which lies 2,000 feet below the Canyon rim, inhabited by the ancient Havasupai tribe. There was no road into the village and a few brave people were riding donkeys down the steep trails. Of course, some tourists went down in a helicopter to visit the approximately 700 natives who welcomed them. The boys sat quietly beside the pilot and listened intently as he explained the scene below us. The half-hour tour was enjoyable for all of us.

Back in our room that evening, the boys took a shower and got into bed to watch TV while I got into the shower. I came out 10 minutes later to see Kirk jumping from one bed to another. When he fell between them I said: "That was a short flight." I have no sympathy for someone who's breaking a rule. They decided to sit cross-legged on the bed and meditate. I lay on my bed and read as the "Ohmm" got louder and louder. I hoped they would soon get tired and go to sleep.

The next morning we boarded the train to return to Williams. They insisted on raising the windows to let the fresh air in. The train looked like a leftover from old cowboy movies, and we chug-chugged up the mountain with black smoke coming through the open window until Kirk lowered it. There were more children than adults on the train, and we adults were warned that the train would be robbed by outlaws on horseback. When I saw them galloping beside the train, and boarding by jumping from their horses, I gave each boy a quarter to give to the three robbers. The children were excited as the robbers came down the aisle wearing bandannas over their faces with guns drawn, collecting coins in their hats. Will refused to part with his quarter and everybody laughed at him, including the robbers. They dumped the coins into a white pillow case, donned their hats, exited the train, mounted their horses, and galloped away. We adults couldn't stifle our laughter as the kids sat there in awe.

We had dinner in Williams that evening, then packed everything for an early morning departure. As we were speeding down the open road at 70 m.p.h. it felt like we were sitting still because we were the only car visible on the long ribbon of concrete which took us to Flagstaff. We continued down highway 89A to Sedona where we had lunch, shopped for oil paintings of the desert, then headed for the airport in Phoenix.

Mom went to work the next morning, and when I heard heavy rain on the kitchen window while the boys and I were eating breakfast, I ran into the garage and backed out the car to get a free car wash. After we ate, I pulled the car in and gave the boys towels to wipe off the car. I wiped the car roof and told them to finish up while I checked the garage freezer to see what we could have for lunch. Will said, "I want a cheese sandwich with toast." I said, "That's called a grilled cheese sandwich." The boys started hitting each other with wet towels. Will ran outside and Kirk pushed the button to close the garage door. I ran over, pushed the button to open the door, and saw Will hanging on and riding it up. Kirk was in the back seat of the car giving him the "thumbs up" sign. I grabbed Will around the waist and sat him down on the wet concrete floor of the garage. I stooped down, and looking into his eyes, I said, "I'm inclined to delve further into your undesirable behavior and try to ascertain a solution to prevent this problem in the future. Now, what did I just say?" He said, "I don't know. You talk too much." The impact I made on him was practically nil. We definitely had conflicting opinions.

I was getting embarrassed as I sat at the table near the stage where Ms. Bartley, the president of the National Association of Nannies (NAN), was about to present me with a pin commemorative of my twenty-five years of work as a nanny. There were 250 nannies attending the yearly conference at a hotel in Reaton, VA in July 2004. Each of the nine families I'd lived with during my 25 years of childcare gave me a glowing recommendation for my resume, and Ms. Bartley was reading excerpts from them. These statements from former employers made me appear to be Mary Poppins and Super Nanny rolled into one, with a sprinkling of Mother Teresa for good measure. I didn't want to be the braggart, and I had no idea that Ms. Bartley was going to shower me with accolades. I think she was trying to inspire the other nannies to do a good job with their little charges.

Finally, she introduced me to the audience, and as I walked up to the stage, I heard thundering applause. I burst into tears and whispered "thank you" into the microphone. I quickly wiped away my tears and said, "There's something Ms. Bartley doesn't know about me—I love to make people laugh. So I'm going to tell you a joke." Slowly, I began to recite an old nursery rhyme:

Hey diddle, diddle, the cat and the fiddle,
The cow jumped over the moon.
The little dog laughed to see such sport,
And the dish ran away with the spoon.

I paused and looked at the nannies' expectant faces. Of course they recognized the nursery rhyme—but what else was there to the joke?

I resumed: As they were running away, the spoon turned to the dish and said, "I want you to know right now, this is not going to be a long-term commitment." I was hooked on the laughter that permeated the room, and during the week I told several stories about the kids I'd worked with. One of them follows:

Will: "Rachel, do you know my email address?"
Rachel: "No."
Will: "It's www.poopy.com

Rachel: "I feel that I must reprimand you for saying that. It's not funny, it's ridiculous. You mustn't talk like that because people will think you're an impudent little boy. Now, what did I just say about your behavior?"

Will: "I don't know. You say so much I get confused."

Will: "Knock-knock."
Rachel: "Who's there?"
Will: "Olive."
Rachel: "Olive who?"
Will: "Aren't you glad olive you?"

The boys and I were shopping for food one day when I saw bananas on sale for thirty-seven cents per pound. What a good deal! I suggested that we buy twenty-five pounds and take them to their former daycare center. The arduous climb up the hill where the children were playing was worth it when I saw them gobble up the bananas with big smiles. Another nanny was there carrying a one-year-old boy who was wearing cowboy boots. I commented that his feet were growing fast. She said: "Not fast enough, I wish he would get off my hip and start walking." I understood her complaint. I'd carried Will until he was fourteen-months old—and I visited the chiropractor once a month.

Will wanted to lie in the grass and listen to me sing *My Bonnie Lies Over the Ocean*, an old Irish folk song that I used to sing to him when he attended that preschool. I sang it all the way through and he said, "It brings back memories." He was so cute! I hated to see him grow up. On the way home, when they started an argument, I turned up the radio with music to waltz with, and they couldn't compete with that.

Mom came home early that evening to stay with the boys so I could attend a movie at the local library which featured the history of Hunter Mill Road during the Civil War. Kirk wanted to go with me but I thought he might get bored. He promised to cooperate, but I was dubious of his eight-year-old behavior and said, "If you give me trouble you get the Heimlich Maneuver." *Danger Between the Lines* told the story of the struggle between the North and South to protect Washington, DC. We lived near Hunter Mill Road and Kirk was familiar with the commentary in the movie. I was so proud of him for sitting still for an hour. There were no other children present. I got information pamphlets and maps and the next day we took Will and went out to discover the Hunter Mill Road area. They learned to read the map and identify landmarks mentioned in the movie.

Kirk's homeroom teacher called to tell me he had been signing his name in Egyptian hieroglyphs and causing disruptions in the class because the other students were curious. He was continuing to do so after she asked him not to. His gym teacher also called to tell me he wasn't cooperating in class. I assured them that I would talk to him.

After he had a snack, I told him we needed to discuss his behavior according to the teachers' complaints. I was taken aback by his outburst of anger. He said, "Come on! Get real! You and my teachers are picking on me. How much longer will you be here? When are you leaving?" I said, "Don't get your hopes up—I'll be here when you go away to college." He rolled his eyes. I said, "The ramifications of your behavior will be felt far and wide, but mostly on the seat of your pants unless I decide not to tell your mom. I have summarized your story thusly: Just obey your teachers! You better cool it or you will go for your first confession now. You can't wait until you're eight."

Apparently, Will had been listening to us from the next room, and seemed to be a little apprehensive as he looked up at me and said:

"Knock-knock."
"Who's there?"
"Owl."
"Owl who?"

"Owl you know unless you open the door?"

"Knock-knock."
"Who's there?"
"Max."
"Max who?"
"Max no difference. Just open the door."

I think he was trying to cheer me up and I appreciated his kindness. I also needed my upcoming respite in Wilmington, NC where friends had invited me to spend the Thanksgiving holidays with them. My original Edgar Cayce study group started there, and they were still meeting after twenty-eight-years. We looked a little older but were still in good health. We reminisced about the changes that we had gone through since the epiphany we had in 1979. I kept notes for two years on the study group meetings, and later wrote a book titled *Following My Dreams with the Edgar Cayce Readings* which has been in the A.R.E. Library since 1986.

The weather was perfect and we walked on Wrightsville Beach every day. I lived on the beach in Wilmington for two years, for one year in Virginia Beach, and enjoyed it immensely. The time passed quickly and a few friends took me to the airport for my flight back to DC and reality.

The next morning I was driving to school, with my two boys and a neighbor's boy buckled up in the back seat. At eight o'clock on a weekday morning the traffic sends your blood pressure sky-high. I was doing thirty where the speed limit was twenty-five and a car swerved in front of me. Then a taxi pulled out of a side street and blew his horn for me to get out of his way. The boys started a fight in the back seat.

Will: "Nanny, he unbuckled my seat belt."

Nanny: "Buckle it back."

Will: "He punched my arm."

Nanny: "Punch him back."

Will: "He took my lunch box."

Nanny: "Take it back. I wish I had an extra eye in the back of my head."

Will: "Why? So you could see what we're doing?"

Nanny: "No, so I could stare down that guy who's tailgating me."

After delivering the boys at school, I drove home and had a cup of coffee while watching the morning news. Dad called and asked me to get the boys ready to ski in Utah for their Christmas vacation. I said, "They will be ready to go!" That meant I could have a week off—and *I* was ready to go!

The last week of November we celebrated Kirk's eighth birthday with a sleepover for eight boys. I assured the boys' moms that I would be with them every moment from 7 p.m. Friday evening until 10 a.m. Saturday morning. In the TV room, there was plenty of floor space for the boys' sleeping bags. They ate snacks, played games, and conversed while the Power Rangers punched it out on the TV screen. They enjoyed my services as I hurried around the room waiting on them. I knew them personally and enjoyed being with them. At 10 p.m., I told them it was time to wind down. We picked up popcorn that they had thrown at each other and vacuumed the carpet. I showed them how to line up their sleeping bags facing the TV so they could watch *It's a Wonderful Life* with Donna Reed and James Stewart. Of course, I had watched the movie with many children at Christmas time and never tired of it.

The sleeping bags, with boys inside of them were two feet apart, and I told them there was to be no punching or touching each other; it was time to relax. I moved a couch for me to sleep on so I could see every movement they made; but they couldn't see me because they were facing the TV. Mom came downstairs and laughed at my devious method to control (outsmart) eight-year-old boys. Needless to say—they were all asleep within an hour, then they started wrestling at 6 a.m.

I went to the kitchen and started breakfast orders of waffles, eggs, soy sausage, cereal, juice and milk. They gobbled it up and went back to the TV room to play Monopoly and check Kirk's and Will's toys. It was customary in our neighborhood for each guest to bring an unwrapped toy to a birthday party to be donated to the local daycare center. Everyone was happy with that arrangement. The boys' moms arrived at 10 a.m. for coffee and donuts, then took the boys home.

Will and I liked to play the ABC game (which we invented) wherein he lies on a couch, face down, and I draw a letter of the alphabet on his back with my forefinger. He then guesses which letter I drew. He learned the alphabet this way at age four, and a year later he was typing 25 words per minute on the computer.

We also liked to play another game which we invented—"Guess Who"—in which we guessed the names of guests coming to a party from the description given by the hostess. All the guests were well-known characters from preschool books. For example: Someone is walking through the woods wearing a red cape, carrying a basket of goodies, when she sees a wolf. Guess who it is! It's Little Red Riding Hood!

Dad said they wouldn't be able to do laundry while in Utah at a mountain lodge for a week, so the boys and I packed two big duffel bags of clean clothes for them. Kirk packed Harry Potter books and Will packed Sponge Bob and Curious George. They were both avid readers.

While they were in Utah, I told Mom that I wanted to retire so I'd have time to travel with friends. She was very upset because I'd been with her and the boys for six years and she depended on me to manage her household. I assured her that I would stay until she found a competent person to replace me. She started calling Nanny agencies to no avail for two months. Finally, after six interviews with nannies from the DC area, she found a nanny from Michigan who had raised two sons and would be capable of caring for Kirk and Will.

I had my 78th birthday the last week in February and the boys gave me a cake with one large candle. I was in good health and happy about starting a new adventure in Cincinnati, OH where my two daughters lived. I had plans to stay up late reading and eating chocolates, sleeping late, watching afternoon movies, and just listening to the quietness, while I wrote a book about my adventures as a nanny.

March, 2008

Re: Rachel Kendal

Rachel came to live with me and my two sons when Will was eight months old and Kirk was three. For six years, she was like a second mom to them and they adored her. I'm a single lawyer and when I was away from home on business, I trusted her completely in caring for them.

The boys are now in kindergarten and second grade and well above average intellectually, thanks to Rachel's experience with preschoolers. I feel blessed that she was able to stay with us and to give the boys a good start in life.

After Rachel notified me that she wanted to retire, it took three months to find a suitable woman to care for the boys. Then, Rachel stayed two more weeks to help her get adjusted to the household.

We will miss her, but know that she will be happy in her retirement years and we wish her the best.

Mom in Vienna, VA

EPILOGUE

February, 2012

During the four years I've lived in Cincinnati with my daughter, Debra, I've enjoyed being a retiree with ample time to write and socialize with new friends.

I've been active with book clubs, writer's clubs, and teaching dream interpretation classes at the Unity Church. Our condo community clubhouse provides us with exercise, swimming, and dancing plus bridge and billiards.

My next book will consist of interviews with retirees, in which I start by saying "Tell me the funniest story you know." I believe in laughter!

Rachel

Made in the USA
Charleston, SC
19 April 2012